Margrit Mondavi's
Vignettes

Margrit Mondavi's Vignettes

STORIES AND RECIPES FROM A LIFE IN WINE

MARGRIT BIEVER MONDAVI

WITH JANET FLETCHER

For Philip, Annie, and Phoebe

Text by Margrit Biever Mondavi with Janet Fletcher
Paintings and sketches by Margrit Biever Mondavi
Back cover photograph by Sara Remington
Produced and designed by Jennifer Barry Design, Fairfax, California

10 11 12 13 14 WKT 10 9 8 7 6 5 4 3 2 1

ISBN: 978-0-692-46390-1

www.robertmondaviwinery.com

Contents

Foreword

*S*hortly after the publication of her memoir, *Margrit Mondavi's Sketchbook*, Margrit called and invited me out to dinner. This was to be a business meeting, not a social occasion: she had a new book idea to discuss.

We had collaborated successfully on the *Sketchbook*, but it never occurred to me that Margrit would have another book in her. I thought I had elicited all of her best memories during our *Sketchbook* interviews, but no, she had more to share. All of these stories, she told me, involved a bottle of wine in some fashion. They weren't stories about wine, but wine figured somehow in each narrative—in a leading role in some of the tales and as a bit player in others.

Over the course of our pasta dinner at Oenotri in Napa, we established the framework for *Margrit Mondavi's Vignettes*. She would write, and I would gently polish, this collection of untold anecdotes from her extraordinary life. Illustrated with her whimsical art and seasoned with recipes that had personal significance, the book would allow the woman whom many consider Napa Valley's grande dame to reveal a little bit more of herself. I couldn't wait to begin and worried only that her packed social calendar and travel schedule would make for slow going. But the stories emerged rapidly and fully formed, as if she had been composing them in her head for years.

For someone approaching her tenth decade, Margrit has an astonishing memory and a journalist's eye for details. She recalled long-ago events and places in vivid color, from her first thwarted attempt at cooking Thanksgiving dinner to her subterfuge following a facelift; from the exotic camel market in Kashgar to a penthouse hotel suite in London, the setting for a madcap scene with her husband.

It's apparent from these vignettes that Margrit embraces life with enthusiasm, curiosity, an open mind, a love of people, and an unflagging sense of humor. I hope you will enjoy reading her stories as much as I enjoyed hearing them. Most of all, I'm hoping there will soon be another phone call, another pasta dinner, and another cache of stories untold.

Janet Fletcher
January 2015

Vignettes

What Turkey?

In 1950, the United States Army sent my husband, Phil Biever, and me back to Europe from Igloo, South Dakota. We had a brief stay in Maastricht, and then went on to Eschwege, a little town east of Kassel in the American occupation zone, just three miles from the Russian zone. After the war, the Allies had divided Germany into four occupation zones, each one administered by a different Allied country, until Germany could be reunited.

Even then, five years after the war, most American military personnel in Europe did not have their families with them. Our family at the time consisted of Phil, an army captain; our two-year-old son, Philip; and *moi*. My father had been so anti-Nazi that naturally I, too, had anti-German feelings that I could not easily dismiss. I did feel badly for the German people whose houses had been bombed. After the war, the American military requisitioned the livable houses, and the locals were thrown out. But we had to try not to think about that.

The house we were assigned was a small *Einfamilienhaus* (single-family house) that had originally belonged to a teacher. It still smelled like German food—fried onions, maybe—and I found Hitler propaganda in some of the drawers. It was situated on a little hill and was quite bourgeois, with an entry hall, a living room, a dining room, a little kitchen, three bedrooms, and a bath upstairs. It was furnished army style, but we tried to give it a little of our personality with a few personal items and some treasures we could buy on the black market.

There was a thriving black market in those days. The Germans loved our coffee, cigarettes, bourbon, nylons, and whatever other items we could find in the PX. Although it was not legal to resell these things, we all enjoyed this double standard. Prices were cheap in the army stores, and we got an inflated price or sometimes merchandise, like wonderful Meissen china, in return.

Just imagine: a carton of Lucky Strikes cost us a dollar. Cigarettes were rationed, however: two cartons per week per adult. If you really wanted to trade big time, you had relatives ship cartons from home. You could have anything you wanted if you had money. Otherwise, there was nothing. I remember one captain who bought all of the musical instruments he could find, including pianos. He got them for next to nothing and shipped them home.

Another bargain was maid service. All of us twenty-something American women with babies suddenly had German nannies and maids. Now we ladies had time to play bridge, and during these card parties, we all complained about our maids. Gosh, how I miss that help now. Our maid, Frau Hei, had lost two sons in the war. I remember seeing her dip her hand into a can of Crisco in the Officers' Club kitchen. She hadn't tasted fat in so long.

I was trying to learn a lot at once. My English was sketchy and my bridge was lousy. American traditions like Thanksgiving were new to me, too.

And Thanksgiving was coming. My husband wanted us to have a traditional Thanksgiving dinner with friends. There was Lieutenant So-and-So, Captain So-and-So, Major What's-His-Name. The army had ranks, a class system. You didn't need to know any names. Just look at the shoulder tabs for the rank and voilà: "How are you, Colonel?" If perchance you remembered the name, you just added it to the rank.

Everybody accepted our invitation, and I started planning. Our grocery store was the army commissary in Kassel. I studied *Ladies' Home Journal* for tips. For hors d'oeuvres, peel celery and carrots and make little sticks. The dip came in a jar. Take a grapefruit, if available, and spike it with toothpicks. Cut the imported cheese from Holland into bite-size cubes and skewer them on the picks.

Then I learned about the side dishes. Cranberry sauce came in a can and so did the green beans or peas. Luckily we could get good butter and other dairy products from Denmark, so I made a béchamel sauce for the beans and added a jar of drained cocktail onions. Mashed potatoes? Go for it: good Danish butter and cream and a lot of whipping. The salad? I cringe. Did I make one of those awful Jell-O salads with canned tangerine slices in it? Probably. Sweet potatoes I just could not serve. I had tried them at the neighbors' house. They were topped with marshmallows and I almost got sick, so no yams for us.

Our ovens were too small to hold a turkey, so all the American wives had a deal with the Officers' Club kitchen: bring the turkeys in the morning and the cooks there would roast them for you and also give you a jar of turkey *jus*. Fabulous. We bought a fifteen-pound bird, frozen hard. I started defrosting it as soon as I got it home, and the next morning it went to the Officers' Club. I drew so many turkeys for place cards and menus that I can do them today with my eyes closed.

Because it was such an auspicious holiday, my husband let me splurge. I bought six bottles of Blue Nun on the German market. What can I say? It was a rather sugary, nondescript wine, but it was popular and might have been good with the turkey. If I try hard, I can still remember some honey flavor, some of that Riesling taste that can be so delicate, but this was not a great Spätlese or Auslese.

The guests arrived and Phil served drinks: old-fashioneds, Manhattans, whiskey sours. The club was only five minutes away, so Phil jumped in the car to get the turkey while we toasted. We were probably all a little inebriated with anticipation and holiday spirit. And then Captain Biever in full uniform (as the military men were from morning to night) returned—upset, sad-faced, and sorry. There was no turkey for the Bievers in the club kitchen. Somebody else got it without leaving a trace—no *jus* for us, either.

The chef said he would make it up to us. When the commissary reopened the next day, he would get us the nicest turkey and fix it ASAP. Thank you, but now what?

I could find only a canned ham and some canned tuna in our pantry, so we offered our guests ham and tuna fish with mashed potatoes, beans and onions, Jell-O salad, and cranberry sauce. There was plenty of laughter and lots of jokes but no turkey. Fortunately, the wine was a big healer. In about three hours' time we drank all six bottles. Then we turned up the radio. AFN (American Forces Network) always had some good Duke Ellington and Jimmy Dorsey. We danced and painted our little German house red and talked turkey for days to come.

Fresh Pumpkin Pie

When I moved to the United States with my first husband, Phil, learning to make pie was part of my process of assimilation. Fortunately I had multiple copies of the red-and-white-checked Better Homes and Gardens Cook Book *as a guide. Several of Phil's relatives had decided it was the perfect wedding gift. Today, my daughter Phoebe brings the pumpkin pie to our family Thanksgiving, and that's how I learned that fresh pumpkin makes a tastier pie than tinned pumpkin puree. I put a spoonful of unsweetened whipped cream on each slice and pour Robert Mondavi Late Harvest Sauvignon Blanc.*

One 1½-pound butternut or kabocha squash,

    halved lengthwise, seeds removed

1 cup heavy cream

3 large eggs, beaten

½ cup sugar

½ teaspoon pure vanilla extract

1 teaspoon ground cinnamon

½ teaspoon ground ginger

¼ teaspoon ground allspice

¼ teaspoon kosher or sea salt

One 9-inch unbaked pie shell

Preheat the oven to 425°F. Put the squash, cut side down, in an oiled baking dish just large enough to hold it in a single layer. Roast until a knife pierces the squash easily, about 45 minutes. Remove from the oven, let cool, and then use a spoon to scoop the flesh away from the skin. Puree the flesh in a food processor until smooth. Measure out 1½ cups and transfer to a bowl. Reserve any remaining squash puree for another use.

Add the cream, eggs, sugar, vanilla, cinnamon, ginger, allspice, and salt to the squash and whisk until well blended. Pour into the pie shell.

Put the pie on a rimmed baking sheet to catch any drips. Transfer to the oven and bake for 15 minutes. Reduce the heat to 350°F and continue baking until the custard is no longer jiggly when the pie pan is shaken and a knife inserted into the center comes out clean, 40 to 50 minutes longer. Transfer the pie to a rack and let cool completely before slicing.

MAKES ONE 9-INCH PIE

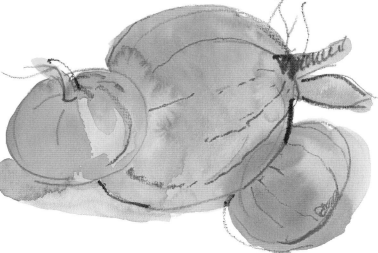

Saving Face

Bob and I often played tennis with Ernie and Virginia Van Asperen. As couples, we made good partners. We bonded through tennis, but we took many skiing and boat trips together. Ernie was a self-made man—he owned a chain of California liquor stores called Ernie's—and Virginia had been a buyer at the Joseph Magnin department store in San Francisco. They were married in the Swedenborgian Church in San Francisco. She hadn't wanted to get married, but Ernie told (*San Francisco Chronicle* columnist) Herb Caen that they were marrying before she said yes. With everyone congratulating them, she couldn't decline.

Virginia had beautiful taste; Ernie didn't. He would listen to Bob's wine talk, but he always knew another wine that was a better deal or another hotel that was half the price. Ernie was fun, however, and Virginia and I liked to be together.

I admired her curiosity; Virginia was interested in everything. She learned to sail because Ernie was always buying or selling a boat. And later, when Ernie got older, she learned how to land their private plane, just in case.

The two of us liked to cook together. Or sometimes we would bring dishes to each other's house—simple things like crab salad with soft lettuces and a homemade mayonnaise with chopped green onions. Obviously, we would drink a Chardonnay with that. She loved fruit pies, so I would often make one. Sometimes we would have a wine tasting—Round Hill (their brand) versus Robert Mondavi.

Virginia and I had chemistry. For years, we met every Saturday morning at the Model Bakery in St. Helena for cappuccino and toasted English muffins. We talked about our friends—maybe it's called gossip—and we made plans. We were the same age, and both of our husbands were thirteen years older, so, naturally, we figured that when they went, we could do what we wanted. We could go to Switzerland together for six months. But then Virginia started not to feel well. It was Lou Gehrig's disease, and it took her in less than a year.

When Virginia and I were in our fifties, we sometimes played tennis with another couple, a Dr. Major and his wife, from San Diego. One day, the four of us had lunch, just the girls and Dr. Major, who was a plastic surgeon. He looked at Virginia and me and said, "You know, I could do something for you."

We laughed and said we never thought about things like that, but later, Virginia and I talked about it. We spoke to Dr. Major again, and he said he would do one of us in the morning and one in the afternoon and give us a good price. We would need to come to San Diego and find a place to stay for three days. Today, this sort of thing is "in and out," but at that time, you were bandaged up.

I was married to Phil at the time, so I asked him, "What would you think if I got a facelift?" Virginia and I didn't call it that, of course. We just said we were going to get fixed up by Dr. Major. Phil replied, "Go for it."

The Van Asperens had a little condo in Coronado where Virginia could stay, but she couldn't take care of me because she would be in the same shape. I remembered a shirttail relation who lived in Fullerton—her name was Ruth—who had always said I should come to visit. So I called and said I was having "a little procedure, nothing special, I won't be in bed." Finally, I said, "Really, it's for a facelift."

A day or two after our visit to Dr. Major's, Virginia and I were bored. But what could we do? We were all bandaged. That's when I remembered Karl Werner. Karl was from Geisenheim, in Germany, and he had made the white wines at Robert Mondavi for a while. We had become friends because I spoke German. Well, it was more complicated than that.

Phil was running for state senator on the Republican ticket, and we went to a fund-raising event at a resort in Pope Valley. There was a group standing around the pool—staid Republicans in gray suits—and suddenly this lovely creature appeared in her bikini and jumped into the water. Later, she reappeared—dressed—and had lunch with us. Her name was Stephanie, and she was gorgeous. Her father was president of the Napa Valley Republicans. She got a summer job with the Robert Mondavi Winery as a tour guide.

Karl was maybe fifty-five and had a wife and several kids, but he fell in love with twenty-year-old Stephanie. I never could understand what she was thinking, but he was a worldly European guy, and she fell for him. One morning he asked me to meet him for coffee. He explained things

and said, "What do you think?" And I said, "Karl, you're meshuga." Well, Stephanie finally came to her senses and went back to school, and Karl eventually took a job at Callaway Vineyard in Temecula. He would often call me to chat and say, "When are you coming to Temecula?"

When I found out that Temecula was less than an hour from San Diego, I called Karl. I said, "Can we see you tomorrow? We don't look very good because we had a car accident and hit the windshield, but Ruth can drive us."

He was totally shocked when he saw us and said, "Oh, I'm just so glad you're alive." And Virginia said, "Yes, this dumb broad stopped too fast."

Karl set up a tasting for us and opened some wonderful wines, mostly big, oaky, old-style Chardonnays, but I must say they were good. Virginia and I tasted through straws. He introduced us to everyone at the winery, saying, "Mrs. Biever and Mrs. Van Asperen had a car accident." And he invited the owner, Bo Callaway, to the tasting, who said, "Oh, you poor things," but I think I saw him wink.

Weeks later, Virginia and I went to San Francisco to get ourselves new outfits at I.Magnin. I remember that I got a reversible raincoat. Afterward, as we walked around Union Square, we noticed men looking at us. And we looked at each other and said, "I guess it worked!"

Dungeness Crab Salad with Avocado and Almonds

Although I always make crab salad by eye and never follow a recipe, this is how I would make it for Virginia if she could still come for lunch. When Dungeness crab isn't in season, I will substitute shrimp, but nothing compares to our sweet West Coast crab. I buy the meat already picked to save time, but you can economize by shelling the cooked crab yourself. Robert Mondavi Chardonnay is almost always my wine choice with crab.

¼ cup sliced almonds

½ pound fresh crabmeat, picked over for shell fragments

¼ cup finely diced celery from the pale inner ribs

¼ cup finely minced green onion, white and pale green
    part only

1 tablespoon minced Italian parsley, plus more for garnish

1 ripe but firm small avocado, halved, pitted, peeled,
    and cut into small dice

3 tablespoons mayonnaise, preferably homemade,
    or more as needed

Kosher or sea salt

½ lemon

Aceto Balsamico di Napa Valley (page 65) or
    other balsamic vinegar (optional)

Little Gem lettuces or hearts of Bibb or butter lettuce

Preheat the oven to 325°F. Spread the almonds on a rimmed baking sheet and toast until fragrant and lightly colored, about 10 minutes. Pour onto a plate and let cool.

Put the crabmeat in a bowl. Add the celery, green onion, parsley, avocado, and just enough mayonnaise to moisten. Toss gently, then season to taste with salt and lemon juice. Add a few drops of balsamic vinegar for depth if desired. Set aside some of the toasted almonds for garnish, then gently fold the remainder into the salad.

Line 4 salad plates with lettuce leaves. Divide the crab salad evenly among the plates. Garnish with the reserved almonds and a little parsley. Serve immediately.

SERVES 4

On-the-Job Training

Harold Griswold (everyone called him Griz) was my mentor in wine and in public relations, and a more straight-up man you can't imagine. He was a Yankee who had swallowed a yardstick. He just had that demeanor, that natural straightforwardness. And people appreciated that he was so direct with them. He treated everyone the same way, no preferences. Everybody had the same rights and could come to him at all times about anything. He set the tone for winery staff, gentle but firm. I admired that and tried to emulate it.

In my early days at Robert Mondavi Winery, I remember a problem with two employees, both of them very good tour guides who were drinking on the job. Today we would call them straight-out alcoholics. I had to say to them, "You can't do that at work. We know you love everything about the winery, but we suggest that you don't drink with the guests. Just lift your glass and toast them and say, 'This will be wonderful with your meal tonight,' but you can't go on five tours a day and drink on every one of them."

George was one of our problems, and he was incorrigible. If there were any dregs of wine left in a bottle after a tasting, he would hide the bottle in the shrubs so he could have a slug between tours. But people loved those tours. The tasting at the end was like a party. Everybody was drinking, George was three sheets to the wind, and it was happiness all over. Wine was spilled, the jokes got bawdy, and it just was not Robert Mondavi Winery style. Griz admonished him, but George would not listen.

One morning Griz said, "Last night I fired George, but look, he's back at work and giving a tour." And there he was, our jolly guide. So that night Griz said to me, "I'm staying late to talk to George again." He told George he was fired and it was no joke, but the next morning George came back to work. I said to Griz, "Would you like me to fire George?" And he said, "Good luck."

I went to the office and had the bookkeeper cut a check with two weeks' extra pay. Then I took George out to the wall by the vineyard. "George," I said, "I know you like the winery very much, but it's not working. I'm so sorry, but it's best that we part. We'll stay friends, but we want to keep the winery shining." And he didn't come back. That experience was, for me, the first little sign that I could do this job.

Griz wanted to retire and he suggested that I would be a good choice to become the new public relations director. Me? I knew I was unqualified, but Griz persuaded Robert Mondavi, who offered me the job. I was nonplussed and declined, but after a lot of coaxing, and with Griz's promise to remain one more year to teach me some tricks, I accepted.

Decades later, there are still employees at the winery who say, "You hired me." Hiring was easy. We sat on the little wall outside, I looked at their CV, and if I felt they had a nice personality and could give a good tour, we shook hands and I said, "Come to work next Monday," and then sent them up to bookkeeping.

There was great camaraderie among the tour guides, who were mostly men retired from other careers. At the end of the day, we would take the unfinished bottles of Chenin Blanc from the tasting room and have a glass of wine together. I had a ball, of course, being the only woman. Often Bob Mondavi would come join us and tell us what he did that day. Everybody would be full of questions for him. This wouldn't happen today. Would you give employees a glass of wine before they drove home? Not anymore.

The tours have changed, too. In those early days, they were much more casual. It was a more innocent time. During the two months that we were crushing grapes, if we took people by the crusher and they were sprinkling sulfur on the grapes, we would explain why. That was before you had to put warning labels on the bottles. Bob responded with a label that talked about wine in moderation, but the government made us take it off.

We did not have many visitors in the beginning. In 1967, it rained for months without stopping. It was one of the worst vintages Napa Valley ever had. Griz always predicted that the day would come when we would have a goose egg—no visitors—but that never happened. The lowest was five.

But the employees loved what they were doing and felt they were working at the best place in the world. Griz wanted the tour guides to have uniforms, and he got Bob to agree to a camel-colored jacket and gray slacks. (I wore a skirt and high heels.) He established the tour pattern. You know, tour guides are the biggest actors. The stories I heard! Sometimes I had to reprimand them and say, "That's going a little too far." At Beringer

Vineyards, one of the guides would tell visitors that an oak tree on the property had roots that got into the tank and drank about 30 percent of the wine each year.

As a tour guide, you saw some strange things. I once watched a woman put her baby down and change it on the tasting table. I remember another time when I had to come in early on a Sunday morning to give a tour. The guests were hung over and trudging along. Afterward, an employee ran up to me and said, "Margrit, there's a big flood." One of the guests—it must have been the last guy in the group—had opened a valve on a tank, and we lost about three hundred gallons.

Another Sunday morning, I was getting ready to give a tour, and I was standing outside under the arch preparing to greet people. That's when I saw a little truck drive out of our parking lot with a sixty-gallon wine barrel on it. I thought, "I wonder where that barrel came from?" After the tour, I went back to the cellar, and the top barrel on the pyramid was missing. I called the sheriff's office but there was nothing that could be done. No sign of the little truck with one oak barrel in back. That's twenty-five cases of wine, and it was our best Cabernet Sauvignon.

In the early years, Griz and I had a system. We would close the tasting room and then go put up the chain at the entrance by Highway 29. I was about to tend to the chain one evening when a little Volkswagen pulled up and four scruffy fellows jumped out. They wore torn jeans and dirty white T-shirts, and they were kind of pushy and arrogant. "We'd like to taste your reserve wines." Well, I said, we don't really make reserve wines but we have some unfiltered wines. They were all gruff and said, "Well, that's good stuff, right?" I got some glasses and they tasted, and then they bought $800 worth of wine and paid in cash. They were from Berkeley. Were they drug dealers? I don't know, but it taught me a lesson: never judge people by their clothes or their cars.

I always told the employees, "Don't say no; say maybe." Don't say, "No, you can't come before ten o'clock." Instead say, "Would you please come later?" Don't say, "No, you can't picnic here." Say, "The Oakville Grocery is just down the road, and the Pometta Deli makes wonderful spit-roasted chicken."

In the beginning, we charged one dollar per person to eat dinner in the Vineyard Room, wine included. Plus, of course, you paid the caterer. I would decorate from Cost Plus. I bought ten-cent candles by the box and stuck them in empty wine bottles. We had so many parties there. The Vineyard Room is surrounded by the To Kalon Vineyard, with the purple foothills of the Mayacamas Mountains in the background. *Pas mal!*

I remember one prominent caterer who had a bad temper and really knew how to curse. He had student waiters from the university, and they wore mustard-colored jackets. One time he made a romaine salad and told each waiter to throw a handful of shrimp on it and add the dressing. There were maybe eighty guests, and after forty servings, there was no more shrimp. "The bastards" had put too much shrimp on the first ones.

The evening went downhill from there. In place of the missing shrimp, the waiters substituted pomegranate seeds, so the lamb had to be made without pomegranates. For dessert, the caterer had made a sort of apple compote in square pans. He took the pans out of the oven and put them on the floor, and one of the waiters stepped in a pan. You have never heard such a primordial scream. He had to be taken to the emergency room.

I knew that the people who didn't get any shrimp were not happy. Then somebody accidentally let the contents of the coffee pot run out into the sink. The guests were screaming for coffee. I made "cowboy coffee"—we boiled it, sieved it, and put it out in a pitcher. All the guests got extra wine because I was in charge of the Vineyard Room, and I had to make up for the disaster in the kitchen.

Another time, a group came in for a wine tasting and dinner. But before dinner was served, they cleared the table of plates and started to gamble. They were throwing dice and betting like it was a casino, so as gently as possible, I threw them out.

We worked with a lot of different caterers, and I watched them closely. I thought the best and most serious was André Mercier, from Oakland. He was a ladies' man and got into trouble with women all over. You couldn't cure him. He was always chasing women, but he made wonderful shrimp Provençale. When he made that, we forgave him everything.

Shrimp Provençale

I no longer have a clear memory of André Mercier's shrimp Provençale, except that he used a great deal of garlic. My own appetite for garlic has diminished over the years, so my version is a little more polite. A splash of Pernod or pastis adds that South-of-France taste. If you don't keep this liqueur on hand, try to borrow some, as it is important to the overall flavor of the dish. Serve the shrimp as a first course with crusty bread, or spoon over rice for a light supper. Open a bottle of Robert Mondavi Fumé Blanc.

24 large shrimp in the shell

2 sprigs Italian parsley, plus 1 tablespoon minced

2 slices yellow onion

1 slice lemon

Sea salt

4 tablespoons extra virgin olive oil

1 large clove garlic, minced

1½ cups grated plum tomato

2 teaspoons Pernod or pastis

6 large fresh basil leaves, torn into small pieces

24 Niçoise olives, pitted and halved

1 tablespoon capers, rinsed and chopped

Peel the shrimp, leaving the tail segments intact and reserving the shells. Devein the shrimp if desired. Refrigerate the peeled shrimp while you make the shrimp stock.

Put the shrimp shells in a small saucepan, add the parsley sprigs, onion, lemon, and 2 cups water, and bring to a simmer over medium-high heat. Adjust the heat to maintain a gentle simmer and cook for 20 minutes. Strain the stock through a fine-mesh sieve into a clean saucepan and simmer until reduced to ½ cup. Season with salt and set aside.

Heat 1 tablespoon of the olive oil in a large skillet over medium heat. Add 12 of the shrimp, season with salt, and cook, turning once, just until lightly colored, about 1 minute per side. (They will cook further later.) Using tongs, transfer the shrimp to a plate. Add another 1 tablespoon olive oil to the skillet and repeat with remaining shrimp. Transfer to the plate.

Reduce the heat to low and add the remaining 2 tablespoons olive oil. Add the garlic and sauté until fragrant, about 1 minute. Add the tomato, Pernod, and reduced stock, raise the heat to medium-high, and simmer briskly, stirring, until the sauce thickens and the flavors merge. Stir in the basil, minced parsley, olives, and capers, then return the shrimp to the skillet and spoon the pan sauce over them. Simmer just until the shrimp are fully cooked. (Cut into one to test.) Serve immediately.

SERVES 4

Minestrone with the Count

Robert Mondavi got to know the Comte de Vogüé on a reconnaissance trip to France in the early 1960s. It was his first trip to Europe, with his wife, Marge, and two sons, and he was totally smitten with the vintners' way of life.

The Domaine Comte Georges de Vogüé is one of Burgundy's crown jewels, in the same family for more than five centuries. The eminent Champagne house Moët & Chandon also belongs to the family. So when Robert-Jean de Vogüé, who was chairman of Moët Hennessy, came to Napa Valley in the mid-1970s to view the progress of construction on Domaine Chandon, France's first investment in California wine, Bob invited him to dinner. The two men had a lot of curiosity about each other.

But where to take a count for dinner? Napa Valley in those days had no restaurants worthy of a French aristocrat, apart from the glamorous new dining room at Domaine Chandon. And in any case, the count had told Bob that he didn't want to go to a chichi restaurant. He preferred somewhere with local color, a hole-in-the-wall.

So a date was set and Bob chose The Depot, a popular spot tucked behind the used-car dealers on Soscol Avenue. If you didn't know about it, you would never find it because there wasn't much of a sign. But everybody in Napa knew The Depot, and people from every walk of life rubbed shoulders there: doctors, lawyers, truck drivers, winemakers. You came in through the back door and sat at tables covered with oilcloth, as I recall. I

can't imagine where the owner found all those mean old waitresses, but at least they were fast. They practically threw the silverware down on the table, and the napkins, too.

At the time, I was a tour guide at the Robert Mondavi Winery, making two dollars an hour. But Bob knew that I spoke French, so he asked me to join the two gentlemen for dinner. I put on my Sunday best and went to the restaurant. By and by, Mr. Mondavi and the count arrived. The count was old-school, polite, charming. It didn't take me long to realize that my services weren't needed at all. The count spoke beautiful Anglo-English.

Bob found a Charles Krug Gamay on the wine list, which arrived ice-cold from the refrigerator. And then, with no ceremony or explanation, the meal began to arrive. The Depot was table d'hôte, always the same: First, the antipasto, which, as I recall it, was not much more than a few slices of salami, a handful of olives, and some crusty bread. Next, a hearty minestrone, with beans and grated cheese. And then the famous tomato-sauced *malfatti*—"badly made" pasta—still prepared, quite visibly, by the elderly grandmother on a butcher-block table in the back. For the main course, you had a choice: chicken cacciatore or transparent slices of roast beef. More silverware would be thrown at you, and the meal would end with ice cream.

The two men started talking about Burgundy and Napa Valley and Domaine Chandon, how groundbreaking it was that a distinguished Champagne producer recognized the Napa Valley for its potential to produce sparkling wine of great quality. Bob, always so full of optimism, spoke of his enormous vision with a speech that I would hear often in the years to come. It always seemed to me to have a bit of Jefferson in it: "Look at this valley. We can grow grapes and make wines here equal to the great wines of Europe. We have the soil, the climate, the *cépages*, the winemaking knowledge. We are progressive. We have new winemaking equipment and new technology. And now you French vintners are bringing us all your great savoir-faire, your tradition. Bravo!"

With the minestrone, the count brought forth a wine, the family's beautiful Chambolle-Musigny. The bottle was a gift for Bob, but Bob insisted we open it. He always liked to compare wines, but of course there was nothing at The Depot to compare with this Burgundy. So he pulled the cork carefully and asked for an empty water pitcher, a real decanter being out of the question. He also asked for extra glasses, but the waitress snapped, "You already have glasses." Finally, a chipped pitcher arrived and some cheap little wine glasses. Bob poured us each a taste.

An aroma of rose petals and violets wafted from my glass. Do I really remember this wine? I shall never forget it. My father had some old Burgundies in his cellar, and as I tasted the Chambolle-Musigny, memories flooded back.

I put on a knowledgeable mien and listened to the fine descriptions of bouquet and texture and taste. For the rest of the meal, the two were deep in discussion, talking about the importance of the vineyards, which wasn't talked about much in Napa Valley in those days. With winemakers, Bob would always ask a lot of questions. And he would say, "If you don't want to tell me, I understand." But Bob himself had no secrets, and he believed there was room in the wine business for everybody. He had no fear of competition. The more good wine that comes from Napa Valley, the better it is for me, he always said. If he was in a restaurant and saw the Cakebreads at the next table, he would say to the manager, "You know that's Jack Cakebread. You should have his wine on the list. It's really good!" Bob was widely admired for that spirit.

There was an immediate chemistry between Bob and Robert-Jean de Vogüé, and by the end of the evening, I was in love with both of them. They couldn't talk enough about each other's passions and about trying something new. Those silly little glasses were refilled until the bottle's last drop, until even that dry roast beef became delicious.

Fennel and Celery Root Soup

In my childhood home in Switzerland, the main meal of the day always started with soup. It might be a light brodo with my mother's veal dumplings or a vegetable potage. I still delight in a well-made soup, and although I enjoy minestrone, I like purees even more. They remind me of the something-from-nothing soups that my mother would magically produce from whatever lurked in the vegetable bin. You can improvise with this recipe. Substitute carrots, mushrooms, turnips, broccoli, cauliflower, or peas for some or all of the fennel or celery root.

2 tablespoons unsalted butter, plus more for garnish

1 medium yellow onion, chopped

2 medium fennel bulbs, stalks discarded, bulbs coarsely chopped
    (no need to core)

1 small celery root (celeriac), about 1 pound,
    peeled and coarsely chopped

5 cups chicken broth, plus more if needed (if using canned broth,
    use half broth and half water)

Kosher or sea salt and freshly ground black pepper

Finely minced Italian parsley for garnish

Melt the butter in a heavy pot over medium heat. Add the onion and sauté until softened, 5 to 10 minutes. Add the fennel, celery root, and broth and bring to a simmer. Cover, adjust the heat to maintain a gentle simmer, and cook until the vegetables are completely tender, about 30 minutes.

Remove from the heat and let cool slightly. In batches, puree the soup in a blender or food processor. Return the soup to a clean pot and reheat gently, then season with salt and pepper. If the texture is too thick for your taste, thin with additional broth.

Divide the soup among warmed bowls. Garnish each portion with a thin slice of butter and a sprinkle of parsley. Serve immediately.

Serves 6 (makes about 8 cups)

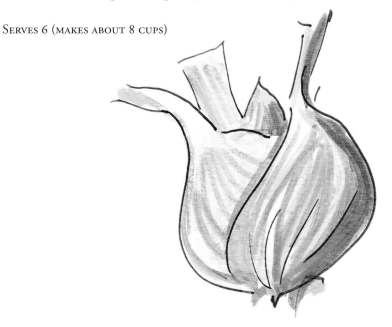

Burying the Cabernet

I have lived in twenty-one different homes in my life, not counting school dorms. I don't know how I managed. When I was married to Phil and he was in the army, we were always half-ready to get orders to move. Certain possessions I would carry from place to place: my Rosenthal china, my silver, and some objects that my parents gave me. But the army furnished everything else. I knew how to sew, so I would make a special bedspread and matched curtains for each new home.

Living with Phil, I always had dreams of a house that was just a little bit better, but he didn't share them. When you have lived through the Depression, as he did, you pinch every penny. With Bob Mondavi, it was the other extreme. I had to hold him back. He thought you should spend your last dollar on the undertaker and drink your last fine wine the day before you go.

After my divorce from Phil, in the fall of 1979, I lived for a few months in a spec house on the top of Spring Mountain in St. Helena. It had never been lived in, and I hardly lived in it, either. I used the bedroom and the kitchen and not much else. It was not the happiest time in my life but thankfully, it was brief.

By the spring of 1980, Bob and I were married. We paid $76,000 for a twelve-hundred-square-foot condominium on Mariposa Street in St. Helena. It was cute and just right for the middle-aged couple we were: happy, newly married, and in love. It had two bedrooms and two bath-

rooms and a fireplace in the living room. I loved that little condo and Bob did, too. I had a hard time leaving it.

But Bob had never owned a home in his life—he had always lived on company property—and he wanted to build his dream house. The site he had in mind was just above Yountville but inaccessible, at the top of a wild, rocky hill. So one sunny day Bob and I borrowed a Jeep and tried to find a way up. It was almost impossible to beat a path through the wilderness of poison oak, blackberries, and other brambles. We got out of the Jeep and climbed the last stretch until we got to some big rocks. There are a dozen of these volcanic cones in the Napa Valley, and the one on this hill was the highest, an ascension point. Surely the Wappo sent smoke signals from this spot, probably greetings and alarms.

The Wappo were an indigenous tribe possibly connected to the Pomo. They had no written language, and they lived by the Napa River. The river had so much salmon that the Wappo didn't even need to fish. They could haul them in with a net or with bare hands. They ate birds, deer, acorns, and whatever other delicacies they could find.

The Napa Valley was home to several Wappo villages when the Mexican missionaries arrived in the early 1800s. Tragically, the newcomers chased the Wappo up to Lake County, where they succumbed to every white man's disease and soon disappeared. Fifty years ago, when I was asking around, I heard that there was still one person in Santa Rosa who was half Wappo. During the construction of our house, I found obsidian arrowheads and stone bowls, which I hid under a big rock. I thought I would display them inside the house once it was completed, but some of the construction workers must have found my treasures. They probably thought some Wappo had left them there.

I had prepared a picnic for us on the day that Bob and I first climbed up there: his favorite roast chicken. I would just whack a bird into quarters, rub it with lemon juice, and season it with salt, pepper, and some rosemary. I baked it in a hot oven until the skin was crispy and the meat yielded delicious juices to mop up. I probably also made a Swiss potato salad. I used yellow potatoes, boiled and cut into thin slices, good olive oil and wine vinegar, some chopped yellow onion or green onion, coarse sea salt and pepper, and finely chopped parsley for color. And I probably brought imported cheese from the Oakville Grocery—some Fontina or Roquefort—and some peaches and apricots. The Swiss bakery in St. Helena had good bread. Bob always said *senza pane non si mangia.* (It's not a meal without bread.) We had a tarp, two plates, two wineglasses, and a bottle of the famous 1974 Robert Mondavi Cabernet Sauvignon.

We sat on those big rocks where the Wappo must have sat, and we imagined the house: the kitchen facing west, toward the Mayacamas hills; the living room with the indoor swimming pool facing south, toward Napa and San Francisco Bay; the bedroom facing east to the Stag's Leap palisades. Those hillsides will be pink at sunset and sparkling silver at sunrise. (We were later famous for building a big house with only one bedroom.) The entrance will look north, with a view of vineyards all the way to Mount St. Helena in Calistoga. Some old oak trees will have to be sacrificed, but we will keep as many of these dear friends as possible.

Bob and I were enchanted by the view from the site and by our daydream. We were finally married, together at last *per sempre*, and it was time to pull the cork and sip the wine. Bob always said he wanted his Cabernets to be "as soft as a baby's bottom, with the power of Pavarotti." The wine should be friendly, balanced, with fruit that spoke of its provenance, the acclaimed To Kalon Vineyard of Oakville.

One of Bob's favorite adages was, "Everything in moderation with glorious exceptions." And this day was indeed glorious. The wine was powerful but smooth, with hints of cassis and layers of flavor. We kept on toasting: to the house, to us, to life. We toasted so energetically we broke a glass. And then the bottle was empty.

I found some flat stones and we had two forks. The soil was hard but we dug and dug until we had a hole big enough to accommodate the bottle. We signed and dated the bottle and buried it with decorum, like a time capsule. It felt like the beginning of so many things—not just the house and our marriage but also how we were going to structure our lives in terms of work and play and travel. We knew there was much to do: engineering a road, building the house, choosing the furniture, and fun things like finding bells for the tower. It took a year and a half just to build that road, even though it was only a mile and a half long.

When construction on the house finally ended, I remembered a Swiss tradition. I cut a five-foot tree and hung red ribbons on it, and then the workers put it on the bell tower as a symbol that the roof was up. I asked the contractor if his crew could have a little time off for a celebration. And so we had a big picnic on the terrace for twenty or thirty workers, with a quarter chicken and a slice of chocolate cake for each of them.

When the house was ready for visitors, we had a celebration combined with the release of the first Opus One, the joint venture between Robert Mondavi Winery and Château Mouton Rothschild. The 1979 and 1980 vintages were released together so that we had enough of these prestigious wines to make a little splash. This was to be a chichi event, with Baron Philippe de Rothschild at the top of the guest list. Bob wanted me to create a nice invitation, so I made a little sketch of the house and wrote, "You are cordially invited to Wappo Hill. . . ."

When I showed Bob the concept, he said, "What's Wappo Hill?" And then he put his foot down. "No, you can't name it Wappo Hill," he said. "I grew up in the hinterlands of Minnesota, and I was a wop and a dago. People will say, 'That old wop built himself a house.'" But by and by, Wappo Hill stuck.

Bob loved the house. He swam in the pool every day. We had a fireplace in the kitchen and a fire going all the time. Bob didn't know how to boil water, but he liked to build fires. And he was the most wonderful meat carver I ever saw, like a surgeon.

Bob and I ate simply when we were alone, maybe a little thin soup with vegetables and then chicken or fish. He loved my fresh tagliatelle, and he would help me drape the pasta on the drying rack. I would make a veal stew with mushrooms and carrots, and he liked to have that with pasta. More and more, I prefer pasta with a simple fresh tomato sauce, cooked in twenty minutes, with good olive oil, shallots, and basil. I'm not big on garlic.

When it was just the two of us, we ate in the kitchen or on the terrace. Or I would pack our dinner in a basket and we would eat in the garden. That came from my parents. They would eat anywhere but in the dining room.

Creating our home on Wappo Hill was the start to our married life and, you must believe it, we never argued. Why argue? Life is too short, and no one wins an argument anyway. Instead, we said, let's discuss the issues, listen to each other, and make every day fun, beginning with a picnic and a special bottle buried in the rocky soil of Wappo Hill.

Bob's Roast Chicken

In the years before the Robert Mondavi Winery had a chef on staff, I roasted a lot of chickens in the winery kitchen. I would chop the whole bird into quarters first so it cooked quickly and was easy to serve, and I rarely did anything more than rub it with olive oil, lemon, and herbs. (Sometimes now I am lazy and just lay whole herbs on top.) Bob loved to mop up the juices with chunks of fresh bread. And although he appreciated haute cuisine and dined in many grand restaurants over the years, I could not make any meal that would please him more than my roast chicken with a bottle of his Cabernet Sauvignon Reserve To Kalon Vineyard.

1 whole chicken, 3½ to 4 pounds

1 large lemon, halved

1 tablespoon kosher or sea salt

Freshly ground black pepper

1½ teaspoons minced fresh rosemary, or 4 sprigs rosemary,
    each 4 inches long

1½ teaspoons minced fresh thyme, or 4 sprigs thyme,
    each 4 inches long

Preheat the oven to 425°F.

Cut the chicken into quarters (2 drumstick-thigh pieces and 2 breast-wing pieces), or ask the butcher to do it. Save the backbone for broth. Squeeze lemon juice all over the chicken.

In a small bowl, combine the salt, several grinds of black pepper, minced rosemary, and minced thyme. Season the chicken all over with the mixture. Alternatively, season the chicken with just salt and pepper and lay sprigs of rosemary and thyme on top.

Set a flat rack inside a rimmed baking sheet. Arrange the chicken pieces, skin side up, on the rack. Roast until the skin is well browned and crisp and the juices run clear when a thigh joint is pierced, about 50 minutes. Let cool for a few minutes before serving.

SERVES 4

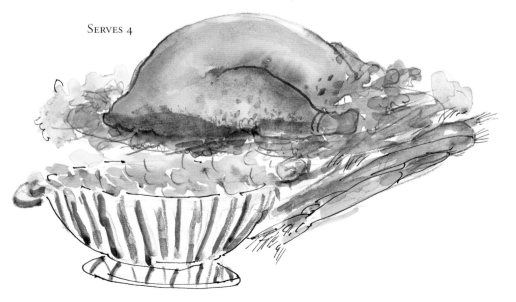

Swiss Potato Salad

In Switzerland, potato salad was the side dish of summer. We ate it with roast chicken, grilled meat, and bratwurst—sometimes with tomato salad, too. I never saw it for sale in any shop; every home cook knew how to make it. We had only one kind of potato, a dense, yellow potato that you could boil and cut into neat slices. We never added chopped eggs or celery or mayonnaise. Why would you do that to those lovely potatoes? My mother made our potato salad with only olive oil, red wine vinegar, chopped onion, and parsley, and it was so good. It held up nicely overnight in the refrigerator. Mayonnaise was for fried fish.

2 pounds waxy fingerling potatoes or Yukon Gold potatoes

3 tablespoons extra virgin olive oil

1 tablespoon red wine vinegar, or more to taste

1 teaspoon Robert Mondavi Cabernet Sauvignon (optional)

⅓ cup minced green onions, white and pale green parts only

2 tablespoons minced Italian parsley

Kosher or sea salt and freshly ground black pepper

Put the potatoes in a large saucepan and cover generously with salted cold water. Bring to a simmer over high heat. Cover partially with a lid and adjust the heat to maintain a gentle simmer. Cook until a knife pierces the potatoes easily, 15 to 30 minutes or more, depending on size. Drain and peel as soon as you can hold them comfortably. (The potatoes are easier to peel when hot.) Let the peeled potatoes cool completely before slicing.

Slice the potatoes thinly, halving them lengthwise first if they are large. Put the sliced potatoes in a large bowl and add the olive oil, vinegar, wine (if using), green onions, parsley, and salt and pepper to taste. Toss gently to avoid breaking up the potatoes, then taste and adjust the seasoning. The salad will probably need a little more vinegar. Serve immediately or leave at room temperature for up to 4 hours. Taste and adjust the seasoning again before serving.

Serves 6

Veal Stew with Celery Root, Carrots, and Pearl Onions

Bob and I treasured the evenings that we were home alone together. He was the least-domestic man I ever knew and could not have put breakfast on the table, but he was not hard to please. Pasta always made him happy, and he liked my veal stew.

Veal was common on Swiss tables when I was growing up, and my mother prepared it beautifully—veal roasts for special occasions, veal stew for every day. Her stew was heavenly because the veal was so tender. She would add mushrooms in autumn, or tomato, basil, and garlic in summer. We would have noodles, rice, or mashed potatoes with it, and I must say her mashed potatoes were marvelous. There was no holding back on the butter or cream, and nobody was ever on a diet.

I have always made stew with boneless veal shoulder, but I have noticed in recent years that the veal in butcher shops is not what it used to be. The cubed meat labeled "veal stew" sometimes makes such a tough, dry braise that I wonder what part of the animal it came from. Talk to your butcher a few days ahead and make sure you can get boneless shoulder. An even better choice, if you don't mind bones, is veal shank cut for osso buco. Ask for the smallest pieces and you will produce a succulent stew. Enjoy with Robert Mondavi Merlot.

24 pearl onions

3 pounds veal shank cut for osso buco, or 2 pounds boneless
    veal shoulder, cut into 1-inch cubes (see recipe introduction)

Kosher or sea salt and freshly ground black pepper

2 tablespoons unsalted butter

1 tablespoon extra virgin olive oil

½ cup dry white wine

½ cup chicken broth

1 large sprig rosemary and 6 sprigs thyme, tied together with
    kitchen twine

2 cups cubed peeled celery root (celeriac), in ³⁄₄-inch cubes

½ pound carrots, peeled and sliced on the diagonal
    about ½ inch thick

1 cup frozen petite peas

1 tablespoon all-purpose flour

2 tablespoons minced Italian parsley

Bring a saucepan of water to a boil over high heat and have ready a bowl of ice water. Boil the onions for 1 minute, drain, transfer to the ice water, and let cool. Drain, then peel the onions, removing the papery outer layers. Trim the root end of each onion but leave intact, so the onion will hold together.

Season the veal all over with salt and pepper.

Heat 1 tablespoon of the butter and the olive oil in a broad, heavy Dutch oven over medium-low heat. When the butter melts and begins to foam, add the onions and cook, stirring occasionally, until they are browned in spots, about 10 minutes; do not allow the butter to burn. Using a slotted spoon, transfer the onions to a plate, leaving the fat behind in the pot.

Add half of the veal to the pot and brown over medium heat on all sides. Adjust the heat as needed so the meat browns nicely without scorching and without burning the butter. As the pieces are ready, transfer them to a plate and continue with the remainder of the veal.

When all the veal has been browned, pour off any fat in the pot and return the pot to medium-low heat. Add the wine and simmer until reduced by half. With a wooden spoon, scrape up any meaty residue stuck to the bottom of the pot. Add the broth and ½ cup water. Return the veal to the pan along with the herb bundle, tucking the herbs down into the liquid. Bring to a simmer, cover tightly, adjust the heat so the liquid barely bubbles, and cook for 1½ hours.

Add the onions, celery root, and carrots and moisten them with the pan juices. Re-cover, adjust the heat so the stew simmers very gently, and cook until both the meat and the vegetables are fork-tender, about 30 minutes longer, stirring gently from time to time so the vegetables cook evenly. Add the peas and continue to cook, covered, until they are hot throughout, about 5 minutes. Remove and discard the herb bundle.

Put the remaining 1 tablespoon butter and the flour in a small bowl. Blend with a spoon or your fingers until completely smooth. Stir this mixture into the stew and simmer until the pan juices thicken slightly, about 2 minutes. Stir in the parsley. Taste and adjust the seasoning. Serve immediately in warmed shallow bowls.

SERVES 4 TO 6

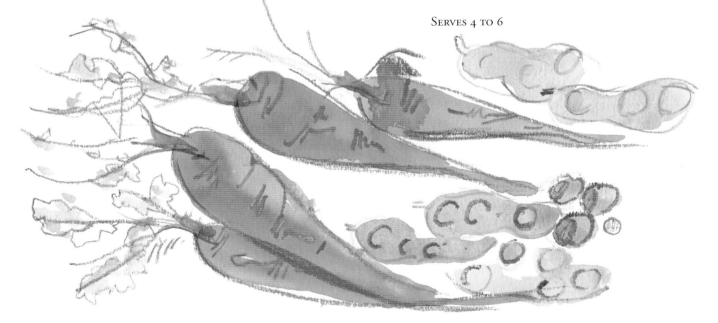

No Room at the Yurt

During the 1980s, the first decade of our marriage, Bob and I went on several trips to Asia with our travel guru, Bill Wu. Bill was a professor of Asian art and culture at Princeton University. When he planned a trip to Asia, we were always the first to sign up. Bill was a gourmet and a seeker of the exceptional. He found places nobody else could find. Even under Communism, Bill could find good Chinese food.

We went to Vietnam, Laos, Indonesia, Burma (now Myanmar), Cambodia, and Bali with Bill, and to China several times. Bob thought of these journeys as university courses, with Bill as our teacher. These were not easy trips, but we were adventurous. There was nothing we wouldn't do.

The most memorable expedition we took with Bill was to western China, following Marco Polo's footsteps. The culture was more Islamic or Middle Eastern than Chinese, with foods like lamb cooked in yogurt with mint. I do believe this was the most adventurous trip Bob and I ever took. We rode on planes, trains, jeeps, horses, donkeys, and camels. On one little plane, I told the attendant my seatbelt was broken, and she said, "That's okay!"

I will never forget the recalcitrant donkey that Bob had to ride. Bob Mondavi, who could conquer the world, never conquered this stubborn, stupid ass. It wouldn't move. It just went into a ditch and stood there. We finally got Bob off the donkey and onto a horse.

One of our stops was in Turpan, probably the largest grape-growing region in China. Marco Polo mentioned the fine grape wine from this area.

White grapes, for the table, for wine, and for raisins, were grown. The fruit dryers looked like beehives in the vineyard. What a brutal place for grapes. In summer, the temperature could be well over 100°F; in winter, zero. The farmers had to bury the vines for the winter.

Our motel in Turpan was brand new, and in the style of the times, you had to climb over construction material, trenches, and wires. We were probably the first guests in our room. The wash basin was smaller than the hole the construction workers had cut for it. When I touched the faucet, the sink fell through the hole and shattered. Water everywhere! Everybody at the front desk spoke Uighur, but I finally got some poor clerk to look at the mess, and we got a new room where the basin fit the hole.

The next day we started our journey to visit a winery, a three-hour-plus trip through the Taklamakan Desert. Of course the bus broke down, but eventually we were rescued. I believe some repairs were made with glue from minced raisins. When we had to have a pit stop, the driver would find a ditch with a few bushes. These "facilities" had been used since the days of the caravansaries. We would look for a clean bush, and voilà: *une toilette*.

It was a long trek in the desert, but then suddenly, like a Fata Morgana, a structure with some vineyards around it emerged. As usual, we stumbled over construction materials, mud, piles of odd bits of metal, and rolls of barbed wire to the entrance, where a friendly group of hosts greeted us with deep bows and wide smiles. They were expecting Robert Mondavi.

At the time, the Chinese government was interested in the possibility of a joint venture with Robert Mondavi Winery, maybe along the lines of Opus One. We had started our trip in Beijing, and while the rest of the group stayed in a hotel, the government wanted Robert Mondavi to stay in a government guesthouse. It was a horrible, dusty, dark place with burgundy velvet chairs. Bill Wu came with us to interpret, and we had a couple of discussion sessions. Bob was open to the idea, and he told the Chinese to send one of their winemakers to the Robert Mondavi Winery. But shortly afterward, Tiananmen Square happened, and we never heard from them again.

Our winery hosts had done their homework. They had some background on Bob and they had his picture. We were led to a changing room for a metamorphosis. All of us had to put on floor-length white surgical gowns and caps to tour this mess of a winery. We had to hold our sides to keep from laughing. They led us through the crushing and fermenting facilities, where the tanks were encrusted with sugary sap and the flies were having a ball. Upstairs, we passed through a facility where workers were bottling orange soda pop in those plastic bottles that choked the whole Chinese landscape. The wines were aged in big amphora-type vessels as well as in wooden barrels. We never got to taste them.

We left our gowns back in the changing room and proceeded to a lunch of lamb, rice, and yogurt. We had brought some wine as presents, so we left our hosts with several bottles of 1978 Robert Mondavi Winery Cabernet Sauvignon Reserve. The local wine served with our meal was a sweet, high-alcohol plum wine served in thimbles. *Ganbei!* Down the hatch. It means "bottoms up" and you must.

Our host spoke some English, and Bob persuaded him to open our Cabernet, which was served in those tiny shot glasses. So it was *ganbei* again while Bob talked about the provenance of the grape, the French barrels, the middle body, the bouquet and balance. He told them, as he told everyone, that good Cabernet should have the softness of a baby's bottom and the power of Pavarotti. Then it was back on the bus for a drive through the Gobi Desert to Turpan. We had a lot to talk and laugh about on the ride back, from the ridiculous surgical gowns to the *ganbei*. We had made some Chinese friends, and plum wine can be quite nice. But, maybe, the Cab should have come first.

Then it was on to Kashgar. Nothing in my life was ever as biblical as the dirt-floored camel market there. Its marvels are once-in-a-lifetime: spices, honey, fruits and vegetables, meat covered with flies hanging on hooks. For ten cents you could ride all day on a flatbed truck pulled by mules. That was the public transportation. I bought two rugs there. One is still in my bedroom, a blend of Russian and Chinese design, a rarity today. So much to buy, but how to get it home?

I also bought little fur caps for my family. I'm sure they were from endangered animals and against the law. We stuffed them into duffel bags, and the smell from those fur caps was horrendous. When we got back to our home on Wappo Hill, I hung the caps on trees to air out. Coyotes tore them down, and in the morning, I found furry shreds all over.

The next day we rode in jeeps to Lake Karakul, which stood at more than ten thousand feet above sea level and was surrounded by mountains. There was no road, though it was in the process of being built, and a lot of dynamite had been used to clear the path. For eight hours we hobbled along, and my head got many bumps from hitting the roof. And of course there was no hotel. We were going to sleep in yurts, six to a yurt.

Well, the manager had double booked the yurts, and a group of French climbers coming from Afghanistan was due to arrive any minute. So we were ordered to go to bed at four in the afternoon and pretend we were sleeping. Somehow the poor chap explained the dilemma to the adventurers from France. He found them an auberge eight hours away in Kashgar, down the nonexistent road through the dynamite explosions.

Finally, the yurt keepers let us get up and they cooked something like goat or yak over a fire. We had one bottle of 1979 Cabernet Sauvignon Reserve left. We shared it all around, freezing cold, sitting on logs near our three yurts. Later, we went to sleep on little cots, and it was so cold, we didn't take our clothes off.

We had left most of our belongings at the hotel in Kashgar because we were staying at the lake for just one night. You really couldn't stay longer because you couldn't wash. The lake was still slightly frozen in June, so to brush our teeth and wash our faces, we had to break the ice sheets on the surface. In the morning, we had tea and flatbread.

Eventually Bill Wu bought property in China and thought he would spend half his time there. He felt like he had returned to his roots. But then he got lung cancer, though he had never smoked, and he collapsed in a hospital in Shanghai. If Bill were still alive, I would be traveling with him. For me, travel is a way to live history, and Bill was the ideal teacher: archaeologist, storyteller, and best friend.

Sweet Seventeen

Bob and I were middle aged when we married, so I wanted every anniversary to be special. We might not have that many. He was a romantic and always sent me two dozen red roses and the sweetest cards, but like many men, he did need to be reminded.

In 1997, our seventeenth year of marriage, I realized that our anniversary—May 17—fell on a Saturday, so I started planning. I drew a whimsical invitation with lots of red hearts and made a list of 17 guests. We would start the party at the 17th hour. We would have 17 violinists. In reality, I could only find seven, but we had ten more musicians in the dance band. "La Vie en Rose" was the first of 17 songs they played.

It was hot that evening, hotter than usual for May in the Napa Valley. We gathered on the balconies and terraces of Wappo Hill, our home, and a flag with a big "17" was unfurled from the tower. Michael Chiarello was our chef, and he prepared 17 courses. Of course we counted all the hors d'oeuvres, and we counted the bread and butter and the coffee, too. Many of the seven couples were fellow vintners: the Chappellets, the Coppolas, the Davieses of Schramsberg, the Van Asperens of Round Hill. Maria Manetti and Stephen Farrow came, as did the Deanes. Robbie Deane is a painter and one of the great artists of the Napa Valley. We also invited Bobbie and Tony Cortese; we had been married in Bobbie's home in Palm Springs before her first husband, Harry Serlis, passed away. I believe the solo guest was our tennis coach, Giuseppe Cammaroto.

And of course we served 17 wines, starting with Schramsberg's fine sparkling wine. The only 1917 wine I could find was a Taylor Fladgate Port, but we had some great vintage Cabernets from our friends and some mighty good Chardonnays, too. We had a table with all 17 wines, so guests could choose. Maybe have a vertical. Maybe mix it up and experiment. Maybe stay with a favorite.

We put a refectory-style table by the pool and decorated it with 17 small glass vases, each with 17 red roses, and 17 fat beeswax candles. (I know that Portland is the City of Roses, but in May, I believe that Napa is a fabulous second.) The name cards had a big "17" on them, and we purchased 17 lottery tickets for guests.

We announced the dinner with 17 swings of the Swiss cowbell. Our friends gave us toasts galore—at least 17, I'm sure—and the musicians played our favorite songs from "Volare" to "Bésame Mucho." After 17 songs we requested 17 more because the party went on and on. We ate heart-shaped savories, passion fruit salad, and a big red heart cake for dessert with 17 roses on it.

Doesn't everybody like to dance? Certainly our guests did. The music was so enticing, so romantic. On this balmy night, everyone just glided outside and danced on the balconies. It was such a lovely scene because everyone was dressed to the nines: the women in pastel silk chiffon, the gentlemen in light-colored suits with dashing rose and turquoise shirts. It was so warm that the men's jackets did not stay on long.

You know that nothing goes as fast as time when you are having a good time. Bob and I were still so much in love, still pinching ourselves that we had managed to be together. The future was bright, full of plans, projects, and travel. Four years prior, when Bob turned eighty, he took advantage of a United Airlines offer: a lifetime pass for first-class travel, with a spouse, anywhere United flew, and it flew practically everywhere. No questions asked, no blackout dates. So for business and for pleasure, we booked trips all over the world. Alas, when Bob passed away, I lost my pass; it was only valid with him.

We had suggested that the party would end at 17 past two. At the appointed time, our guests tiptoed, many of them barefoot, over the rose petals we had strewn by the bucketful on the path to their cars.

And then Bob and I had the house alone. I adore that moment: candles to extinguish . . . the smell of the smoke and wax . . . the million rose petals . . . the remnants of a party. The patina was still there and the moon was shining over the pool. Bob and I just felt so thankful, so lucky, so happy, and we wanted the moment to last.

We got our folding roller bed from the closet and pushed it onto the terrace under the big oak tree. The bed was only a bit bigger than a single, but we loved sleeping outside under a big red-and-white-checkered

down-filled duvet. We had a wonderful bedroom indoors, but we almost always slept outside until November or until the first rain. The wildlife was close: deer, squirrels, birds, occasionally a raccoon. And on a lower branch, sometimes, an owl that hooted in the middle of the night. And on this particular, fabulous, not-to-forget evening, the owl hooted 17 times.

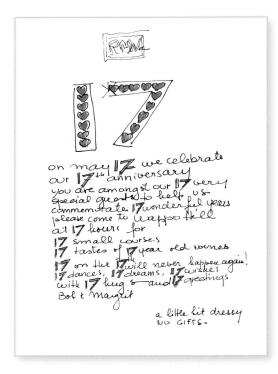

Spinach-Stuffed Quail

I had twenty-eight wonderful years as the wife of Robert Mondavi—a second marriage for both of us. Successful marriages are always hard to predict, especially by those on the outside. Because my older daughter, Annie, was so young when she wed, I was not optimistic, but she and Keith have been together for more than forty-five years. At Annie's request, I cooked their wedding dinner: stuffed Cornish game hens. I don't recall the stuffing, and Annie doesn't have the menu to jog our memories. (She and Keith lost most of their possessions in the big Napa fire of 1981.) I remember serving wilted spinach as a side dish, but I have added it to the stuffing here, and I have substituted quail, which I prefer. Accompany them with wild rice or polenta and Robert Mondavi Pinot Noir.

FOR THE STUFFING:

1 pound spinach

1 tablespoon unsalted butter

1 large clove garlic

¾ cup soft fresh bread crumbs

⅓ cup fresh ricotta cheese

1 tablespoon freshly grated Parmigiano-Reggiano cheese

1 tablespoon chopped fresh basil, or 1 teaspoon chopped fresh marjoram

Kosher or sea salt and freshly ground black pepper

1 large egg, lightly beaten

8 semiboneless fresh quail

Kosher or sea salt and freshly ground black pepper

Extra virgin olive oil

To make the stuffing, discard any thick spinach stems; you should have about 3 quarts spinach leaves. Put the leaves in a large pot with just the wash water clinging to them. Cover and cook over medium heat, tossing occasionally with tongs, until the leaves wilt, about 3 minutes. Drain in a sieve and rinse with cold water. Gather the spinach between your hands and squeeze vigorously to remove as much water as possible. Chop medium-fine.

Melt the butter in a skillet over medium-low heat. Add the garlic and sauté until fragrant, about 1 minute. Add the chopped spinach and toss to coat evenly with the butter. Remove from the heat and let cool.

In a bowl, combine the cooled spinach, bread crumbs, ricotta, Parmigiano-Reggiano, and basil. Mix well, then season to taste with salt and pepper. Stir in the egg.

Preheat the broiler and position an oven rack about 8 inches from the broiling element. Set a flat rack on a rimmed baking sheet. Season the quail on both sides with salt and pepper. Tuck about 3 tablespoons of the stuffing in the cavity of each quail, making sure the stuffing is not exposed. Rub the outside of the quail with olive oil. Place the quail, breast side down, on the rack in the baking sheet.

Broil the quail until the skin is lightly browned and crisped, about 5 minutes. Using tongs, turn the quail over and broil breast side up until nicely browned and crisped, about 5 minutes longer. Monitor closely and be prepared to move the oven rack if the quail are coloring too quickly or too slowly. Let the quail rest for about 5 minutes to allow the juices to settle, then serve.

SERVES 4

An Accidental Penthouse Centerfold

When Bob and I were first starting to date, we often had dinner at L'Etoile, one of his favorite restaurants in San Francisco. It had booths, so it was quiet and private. I still think that's how restaurants should be. Today, most restaurants are a nightmare of noise.

L'Etoile was fun because Peter Mintun played the piano. Peter's father was from Lodi, California, like Bob, and had assembled wooden wine crates with Bob when they were kids. We ate there so frequently that I remember Claude Rouas, the maître d', coming to the table once and saying, "Mr. Mondavi, you cannot have another chicken *forestière*!" But Bob loved it. The food was elegant and delicious, and I would eat chicken *forestière*, too. Bob would order Krug's Réserve Anglaise, a special cuvée. He didn't like Champagne as much as I did—he would rather have had a glass of Cabernet Sauvignon—but he spoiled me. For me, it was always Champagne, which once got me into trouble.

Through wine connections, Bob and I had come to know Anton Rupert, an important businessman in Stellenbosch, the famous South African wine town. Anton was a self-made billionaire who, as a young man, had to drop out of medical school when his family couldn't afford the tuition. He made his fortune in tobacco, and his company eventually owned many luxury brands such as Cartier and Alfred Dunhill. A conservationist, he was among the founders of the World Wildlife Fund. He also was a friend of Nelson Mandela and an outspoken critic of apartheid.

We would always see Anton in London at the International Wine & Spirit Competition. He was very worldly. He had a wonderful flat in Mayfair on Albemarle Street, where Baron Philippe de Rothschild also had a flat, and he had a major collection of South African art. But the most wonderful thing he had was his wife, Huberte.

Huberte was a fabulous woman, with a real instinct about art. Once, when her husband was at a board meeting in Zurich, she learned that a Giacometti collection was being auctioned. She told me, "I had never done this before, but I interrupted the meeting to ask Anton if we should buy it, and he said yes." Huberte was the highest bidder—it went for millions—but then the Swiss government intervened and wouldn't let the collection leave Switzerland. She thought that was the biggest injustice.

One time when Anton was visiting Napa Valley, he noticed a bottle of wine that I had painted with an image of Bacchus. And he said, "Would you donate a bottle like that to our wine auction?" Of course. And when the time came for the auction, Bob and I went to Stellenbosch as guests of the Ruperts. We stayed at their estate, a delightful Dutch colonial–style mansion with a magnificent garden called Fleur du Cap. There was a tree full of ripe mulberries right outside my window.

That trip was when I first learned about apartheid. I got up early one morning and left the estate to walk around, and I found the squatters' quarters below. I realized that this way of life was not perfect, you know?

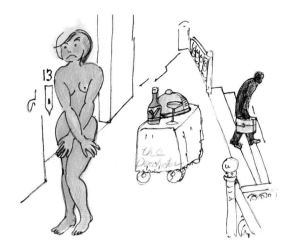

Just beyond our cocoon of luxury were people who were not nearly so fortunate. In Johannesburg, we drove to Soweto where I saw this wonderful fruit stand, and we stopped because I wanted to take pictures of it. At the fruit stand was a little child with a dime. He wanted chewing gum, and the vendor took a fly swatter and swatted at him. I will never forget that.

For the auction, we offered a Robert Mondavi Cabernet Sauvignon 1980, with my Bacchus painted on the bottle. It went for $82,000, an astonishing sum. A crowd descended on us, and we just kept thanking everyone profusely.

The next day, we boarded a long flight from Johannesburg to London, where we would stay overnight. Robert Mondavi wines were just starting to sell in London, and Bob had a business meeting there. The Champagne on the flight was Dom Ruinart, and it was so good, we had more than one glass. By the time we landed, we were as bubbly as the wine.

We arrived at The Dorchester around midnight and learned that the hotel had upgraded us to a penthouse suite. From the corridor you had to climb up a private staircase to a charming, long room. We were so tired, we threw our suitcases in a corner and went straight to bed. All that good Champagne made us sleep well.

I had asked the receptionist to wake us at eight o'clock because I knew that Bob had a breakfast appointment in the hotel restaurant at nine o'clock with Peter Duff, who represented Robert Mondavi Winery in the United Kingdom. When the wake-up call came, I jumped out of bed first to go to the *bagno*. But we had been so exhausted the night before that I hadn't gotten my bearings, and I took the wrong door. It immediately slammed shut behind me, and suddenly I was in the hall without a stitch of clothes on.

There I was, at the top of the open staircase, looking down at a throng of businessmen with attaché cases racing to their appointments. I could not bang on the door because the men would have looked up. All I had to cover my bare self was a little paper flyer promoting Selfridges department store.

Bob did not hear well, so I had to consider my predicament carefully. I heard water running in the bathroom, which meant he was probably shaving. I knew his rhythms. In fifteen minutes, he would go back to the bedroom to dress. So I counted to sixty fifteen times. Then I heard him say loudly, "Margrit, where are you?" I threw my naked body against the door and, lo and behold, he opened it.

"Margrit, God almighty, what are you doing outside without clothes on?"

"Never mind, darling. I'll tell you later. But see? My counting worked."

I don't know how many bankers saw me. Perhaps, if they looked up, they thought their minds were playing a trick, like a hallucination. Or maybe, as Englishmen with great savoir-faire, they diplomatically just looked away.

I got myself together and dressed quickly and joined Bob and Peter Duff in that beautiful old Dorchester dining room for a true English breakfast—those fabulous British eggs with the orange yolks, kippered herring, stewed tomatoes, incredible butter—all served with the skill and discretion of trained English waiters. I glanced around the dining room. Did any of these serious, balding men in their three-piece suits recognize me? I know I look better dressed than bare, but maybe they recognized my hair? I must have looked quite desperate, shivering and counting and holding that ad in front of me.

I knew I could not tell my story at breakfast. Peter was just as stuffy as the other businessmen in the room. Bob, however, in his irrepressible way, said, "Peter, do you know that this morning someone knocked at my door, and when I opened it, there was my wife without a stitch of clothes on?" Peter politely shrugged and excused himself for another meeting.

Bob and I sat with the remains of the breakfast. I said, "Bob, do you realize there were about a hundred men in the lobby who could have had a heart attack this morning?" We started to laugh, and then we couldn't stop. But all's well that ends well. Bob ordered a bottle of Dom Ruinart on the spot, and we sat in that elegant dining room for another couple of hours, enjoying every drop. Back in the suite, I checked the placement of all the doors, especially the one to the loo.

Buckwheat Blini with Smoked Salmon and Crème Fraîche

I am too impatient to make traditional yeast-risen blini, so this faster version with baking soda suits me. You can replace the salmon with smoked trout or offer both so guests have a choice. If you're celebrating or if it's New Year's Eve, splurge on some caviar. The caviar from California's Sacramento River sturgeon is quite good—not Iranian, alas, but at least it's available. Champagne or sparkling wine is de rigueur. Schramsberg Blanc de Blancs never disappoints me, and as a Napa Valley ambassador, I pour a lot of it for guests.

FOR THE BLINI:

¼ cup all-purpose flour

¼ cup buckwheat flour

¼ teaspoon baking soda

¼ teaspoon kosher or sea salt

1 large egg

½ cup plus 3 tablespoons whole milk, or more if needed

2 tablespoons unsalted butter, melted, or more if needed

6 to 8 ounces smoked salmon or smoked trout

⅓ cup crème fraîche or sour cream

Thinly sliced fresh chives for garnish

To make the blini, in a bowl, whisk together the all-purpose flour, buckwheat flour, baking soda, and salt. In another bowl, whisk the egg until blended, then whisk in the milk. Add the dry ingredients to the liquid ingredients and whisk to blend. The batter should be a little thinner than pancake batter.

Heat a griddle or cast-iron skillet over medium heat. When the griddle is hot, brush lightly with some of the butter. Using a tablespoon as a measure, and cooking only a few blini at a time, place ½ tablespoon of batter on the griddle for each blin. The batter should be thin enough for each dollop to spread into a 2-inch circle. Thin the batter with a little milk if necessary. Cook until bubbles appear on the surface and the blini begin to brown lightly around the edges, about 45 seconds. Turn with an offset spatula and cook on the second side until done, about 45 seconds. Taste the first one or two and adjust the heat or timing as needed.

Transfer the first batch of blini to a serving platter. Top while hot with a small piece of smoked salmon, a dollop of crème fraîche, and a sprinkle of chives. Serve immediately. Repeat until you have used all the batter.

MAKES ABOUT 32 BLINI, TO SERVE 8

Sarah Scott's Gougères

Sarah Scott, a Napa Valley chef and former executive chef at the Robert Mondavi Winery, makes the most delicious cheese gougères. I don't understand why these savory cream puffs seem to have fallen out of fashion. Hers are especially crisp and airy and just right with sparkling wine. When Sarah cooks for guests in my home, I almost always ask for gougères to start. She serves them warm, tucked inside a linen napkin.

¾ cup skim milk

6 tablespoons unsalted butter

¾ teaspoon kosher salt

¾ cup bread flour

3 large eggs

¼ teaspoon freshly ground black pepper

¾ cup (3 ounces) shredded Gruyère cheese

1 tablespoon heavy cream

Fleur de sel for garnish

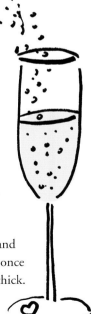

Preheat the oven to 375°F. Line 2 heavy baking sheets with nonstick baking mats or parchment paper.

Combine the milk, butter, and salt in a medium saucepan and bring to a boil over medium-high heat. Add the flour all at once and immediately whisk until smooth. The mixture will be thick.

Reduce the heat to medium and switch to a wooden spoon. (You may have to tap the whisk vigorously against the side of the saucepan to release all the batter.) Cook, stirring constantly, until the batter clears the sides of the pan and loses its raw taste, about 5 minutes.

Remove from the heat and let cool for a couple of minutes. Add the eggs one at a time, beating well and making sure each egg is fully incorporated before adding the next one. Mix in the pepper and all but 3 tablespoons of the cheese.

With 2 spoons, drop walnut-size mounds of batter onto the prepared baking sheets, spacing them about 2 inches apart. You should have room for 12 *gougères* per baking sheet and enough batter for 24 *gougères* in all. Don't worry about making them perfectly neat and round. Brush the tops with the cream and sprinkle with fleur de sel. Coarsely chop the remaining 3 tablespoons shredded cheese and sprinkle on the tops of the gougères, dividing it evenly.

Bake 1 tray at a time until the *gougères* are a deep golden brown, 30 to 35 minutes. (Do not open the oven door while they are baking!) They should be crisp outside and moist but not doughy inside. If unsure, break one open to check. Serve immediately, or let cool on a rack and gently reheat in a 325°F oven until hot, 6 to 8 minutes.

Makes 24

Golden Shoes

For years, Bob had wanted to be asked to the Bohemian Grove, an exclusive men's summer camp near the coast north of San Francisco. It was like a fraternity; you had to be invited by a member. Bob didn't play golf or hang around in bars, but this experience he very much wanted, and eventually the door opened for him. World leaders and top businessmen came to the Bohemian Grove, and they listened to marvelous lectures and put on plays. Bob told me he once played a monk. I don't know for sure what went on there, but I know everyone slept on cots, and I suspect they drank a lot and peed on trees. Women were not allowed except at the Spring Jinks, before the camp started. That's where I met Dr. Luis Alvarez, who had won the Nobel Prize in Physics. I recall that he had a controversial theory about why dinosaurs became extinct.

One summer morning in the late 1990s, when Bob was at the Grove, I got a call from Claude Rouas inviting me to dinner that evening. Claude owned Auberge du Soleil, the beautiful hilltop resort in St. Helena, and he was going to be entertaining a visiting French chef, Jean-André Charial, from the Michelin two-star L'Oustau de Baumanière in Provence. At the last moment, Claude had decided that having another person who could speak French with Monsieur Charial would make the table perfect.

I put on a cute chiffon dress and the gold shoes I had bought the day before in San Francisco. I drove my little car up the hill to Auberge and left it with the valet. I was reintroduced to Monsieur Charial, whom I had met a few years prior when Bob and I visited his restaurant. Some Krug Champagne made the rounds, along with lovely hors d'oeuvres. The view from the terrace was a dream. The balcony of the restaurant has always been one of the best places in all Napa Valley to watch the sun set. But my feet started to hurt, so I sat down on a barstool and played *la dame au bar* with panache.

At dinner on the terrace, I was seated next to the chef, who was charming and interesting. I tried to smile and engage in the conversation, but when your feet hurt, nothing is right. I promised the chef that Bob and I would return to Provence, but what I really was thinking was, "I will never again wear these shoes."

I had brought a bottle of 1981 Opus One—the third vintage—to share with the guests. You must imagine how proud Bob was of this wine and his partnership with the Baron Philippe de Rothschild. It had been years in the making.

❧

When Bob and the Baron first spoke of collaborating, it was like a flirtation. The baron said, "If you have an idea, call me." And Bob replied, "If you have an idea, call me." Six years went by. Then, as he did several times, Bob took a group of winery employees on a European tour. When they stopped at Château Mouton, the baron said, "You never called me." And Bob said, "You never called me."

A few months later, Bob was back for a more serious discussion. He wanted his daughter, Marcie, to see Mouton, so he brought her along, and they each had a room in the château. It was a hot summer day, and when Bob spotted the swimming pool, he asked if he could take a dip. While he was swimming, the staff unpacked his suitcase and put everything away perfectly and washed his socks—very nice, except that Bob had forgotten to pack more socks. So now his only pair was wet, hanging in the bathroom. He talked about those wet socks for a long time.

Over dinner that night, Bob was expecting to discuss business, but the baron did not bring it up. At the end of the evening, the baron said, "I hope, Mr. Mondavi, you don't mind coming to talk to me at breakfast tomorrow in my bedroom. I do all my business in bed."

So the next morning, Bob and Marcie met the baron in his bedroom, and they wrote the whole business plan for Opus One on a yellow pad. How I wish I had that pad. They gave themselves ten years to find land and build a winery that would be nothing like Mouton or Mondavi. Eventually, Susan Pate designed a label with the baron looking west and Bob looking east, which is really the whole story.

❧

The bottle I brought to Auberge was poured around and scrutinized in two languages. A good year . . . *largesse* . . . *goût de provenance* . . . maybe a bit young . . . fine cassis aftertaste. I tried to sound smart and knowledgeable, but how can you when your feet hurt so much? "These shoes will go to Goodwill tomorrow," I thought to myself. "How stupid of me to wear a new pair on an important evening."

We adjourned to the little bar at Auberge where a pianist played wonderful romantic tunes. It was a full moon and the chef asked me to dance. Normally I love to dance, but the pain was worse than childbirth. I thought about the witch in *Blanche Neige* (Snow White), who danced with her shoes in flames. I bit my tongue and had a crooked smile. On the next song, I pretended to be tired.

Coffee was served back on the terrace, and I soon excused myself. "I am alone, Monsieur Charial, and I have to drive myself home, so no more Champagne for me. And, *merci*, no Cognac." I gave my ticket to the valet, and as I waited for the nice young kid in shorts to bring my car, I glanced down. That's when I realized that I had those damned golden shoes on the wrong feet.

I put the top down on the car and drove home barefoot, relieved from my torture, the full moon washing over me. I put those beautiful shoes in my closet and never wore them again. Just looking at them made my feet hurt.

❧

Thai Chicken and Coconut Milk Soup with Kaffir Lime

My mother made an exquisite soup for our family almost every day. For that reason, it seems that I have always known how to take a handful of vegetables, a knob of butter, and some tasty broth and produce a nourishing puree. But this Thai soup was another matter. I first tasted it at Redd, Richard Reddington's lovely restaurant in the Napa Valley, and I had to experiment to get it right. Richard was the chef at Auberge du Soleil—scene of my shoe agony—before he opened Redd. So this is Richard Reddington's soup as made by moi. *You can replace the chicken with shrimp or crabmeat, if you prefer.*

4 cups chicken broth (if using canned broth, use half broth and half water)

1 skin-on, boneless chicken half breast, 6 to 8 ounces

2 tablespoons unsalted butter

½ large yellow onion, thinly sliced

1 can (about 14 ounces) unsweetened coconut milk

3-inch piece lemongrass, cut from the root end,
     halved lengthwise (see Note)

3-inch piece fresh ginger, peeled and halved lengthwise

¼ cup jasmine rice

1 jalapeño chile, quartered lengthwise (remove seeds and ribs for less heat)

⅓ pound mushrooms, sliced or quartered

3 two-lobed kaffir lime leaves, stripped from the stem and
     torn into large pieces

1½ teaspoons Thai or Vietnamese fish sauce, or more to taste

Kosher or sea salt and freshly ground black pepper

1 lime, halved

4 to 6 thin lime slices for garnish

Bring the broth to a boil in a small saucepan over high heat. Add the chicken breast, cover, and remove from the heat. Let stand until the broth is completely cool. Remove the chicken and shred by hand into bite-size pieces.

Melt the butter in a heavy soup pot over medium-low heat. Add the onion and sauté until softened but not colored, about 10 minutes. Add the broth and coconut milk. Smack the lemongrass and ginger with the side of a heavy knife or cleaver to break their fibers, then add them both to the pot. Bring to a simmer, adjust the heat to maintain a gentle simmer, and cook for about 5 minutes. Add the rice and chile and simmer gently, uncovered, for about 15 minutes, stirring occasionally so the rice does not stick to the bottom of the pot. The rice should still be slightly firm.

Stir in the mushrooms, lime leaves, and fish sauce and simmer until the mushrooms are barely tender and the rice is no longer firm, about 5 minutes. Stir in the shredded chicken. Season the soup with salt and pepper and add juice from the halved lime to taste. With tongs, remove and discard the ginger, lemongrass, and chile. Divide the soup among warmed bowls. Garnish each portion with a lime slice and serve.

Serves 4 to 6

Note: To trim lemongrass, cut off and discard the grasslike top and the hard root end. Then peel off and discard the tough outer layer or two of the bulb.

Feasting on the Snake River

In the early 1980s, Bob and I were deeply involved with the American Institute of Wine & Food (AIWF). Julia Child, winemaker Richard Graff, and Bob were the founders of this organization, which had the mission of raising the quality of wine and food in America and making them legitimate areas of study. Once a year, the board of directors got together to celebrate our progress and to discuss future projects for the institute. Crosby Ross, the board chairman, was always full of ideas, and one year he proposed that we go rafting down the Snake River, from Hells Canyon to Lewiston, Idaho.

We were allowed one duffel bag per person, which had to include a sleeping bag, a pup tent, and some Western attire for our last evening together. Of course, this group was always interested in eating well, even on a journey where you were only allowed to leave footprints and take pictures. So in addition to the board members, the entourage included two prominent southwestern chefs—Robert Del Grande and John Sedlar—and sixteen cases of Robert Mondavi wines. We packed Reserve Fumé Blanc and Cabernet Sauvignon, plus some Moscato d'Oro. The muscat is quite pleasant and maybe a little too easy to drink. It's a bit sweet and low in alcohol because the winemaker stops the fermentation before the wine goes dry. It's delicious with fruit desserts and pound cake, and sometimes I serve it frozen. It comes out slushy, like a frappé, and people love it.

We were bused, along with our wines, to Hells Canyon, on the border between Oregon and Idaho. Several dories awaited us there, little boats that held maybe four people each. We packed ourselves into them, twenty serious and important members of the board. The last person aboard was Michael, from the rafting company, with the wine and the toilet.

It was summer, and the river was not too cold. Often Bob and I would take the available rubber kayak and follow the troops in the raft. We learned not to get into eddies and a few other kayak tricks. Of course, we had able young guides to lead us, and if we did get stuck in an eddy, the dory would come fish us out with a big oar.

Lunch was usually casual. Our famous chefs would prepare sandwiches: ham, cheese, tuna fish. There were some crudités, as I recall, and we were allowed a glass of wine or beer. Then we would drift some more and land in a nice spot for dinner and our overnight stay.

I was in charge of table decorations, which usually involved some pretty weeds. The place cards were river rocks. I painted them with the names, date, and place. Some of our friends took the stones with them as souvenirs.

We might have been in the wilderness, but our chefs had brought delicacies: ice chests full of foie gras and caviar. We had facilities for grilling, picnic tables to decorate, and plenty of wine to make a feast on the banks of the Snake River. We sat under the stars, listening to the rushing river, telling stories (some real, some invented), and singing until it was time to pitch the pup tents.

Bob and I soon abandoned our tent. We had always preferred sleeping outside. We inflated our air mattresses and hoped they would stay firm all night. Some of us slept well, some of us didn't, but it was such a fun adventure. Counting stars in that dark sky was just as enjoyable as sleeping.

Every morning it was early up, jump in the river for a swim, pack up, and find your dory. Not surprisingly, there were a few hangovers from the Moscato d'Oro. My friend Barbara and I would admit only to a headache.

There was so much beauty on these trips, so much companionship, and so many friends that we kept forever. And we had some serious discussions about how to make the AIWF grow (which it did), how to upgrade American cuisine, and how to encourage people to enjoy wine in moderation.

Thanks to our chefs, we were not roughing it. We also had a masseuse on board, which was Bob's idea. She brought along a spongy mattress, like an exercise mat, and because we had no tables, she did the massages right on the ground. I remember that massage pad because, on the last evening, we had a Western bash, and we dressed up with bits and pieces of Western wear—whatever we had brought along. Maybe a cowboy shirt or some silver jewelry, a neckerchief or a Western hat. The masseuse cut the

corners off her massage pad so it was oval, pinned plastic chiles all over it, and wore it like a cape. She looked like a taco. It was the showpiece of the evening.

We were getting a little low on wine but still had enough to celebrate this crazy river trip and consolidate our strong belief in a new culture of wine and food for America. And then we had to pack it up. We all went to a motel in Lewiston and took showers—our first shower of the week. Michael was glad to get rid of the toilet. The chefs had nothing left, not even a scrap. The wine had vanished, too, but my memories of this journey remain. Bob and I were always up for adventure, as long as someone brings the wine.

Cognac Pound Cake with Kumquat Compote

My mother rarely baked cakes or pastries beyond an occasional apple tart or kugelhopf, which is like a pound cake with yeast. With so many fabulous pastry shops in Switzerland, why would she bother? So I didn't learn to bake until I came to America and needed to make birthday cakes for my children. Everything I tried from American recipes was too sweet for my taste. Even today, I can't bear sweetened whipped cream. I think whipped cream should be au naturel.

I do enjoy a nice, plain American-style pound cake, although I think a splash of Cognac in the batter improves it. For guests, I'll serve thin slices with a little fruit sauce, whipped cream, and a glass of Robert Mondavi Moscato d'Oro, which is lovely with fruit desserts. In spring, I'll make a strawberry-rhubarb sauce or cherry compote for the cake; in summer, I'll use raspberries. But in winter, I like a compote of sliced kumquats, which have the same orange-blossom scent as the wine.

FOR THE POUND CAKE:

1 cup unsalted butter, at room temperature

3/4 teaspoon kosher or sea salt

1 cup plus 2 tablespoons sugar

4 large eggs plus 1 large egg yolk

2 tablespoons Cognac or other brandy

2 teaspoons pure vanilla extract

Finely grated zest of 1 lemon

2 cups sifted unbleached all-purpose flour (see Note page 58)

FOR THE COMPOTE:

2/3 cup sugar

1 cup water

1/2 pound kumquats, thinly sliced and ends discarded

Cognac or other brandy (optional)

Unsweetened whipped cream for garnish

To make the cake, preheat the oven to 325°F. Butter and flour the bottom and sides of a 9-by-5-by-3-inch loaf pan.

In a stand mixer fitted with the paddle attachment, beat the butter and salt on medium speed until very creamy. Gradually add the sugar and beat until light and fluffy. Add the eggs one at a time, beating well after each addition until fully incorporated. Add the Cognac, vanilla, and lemon zest and beat until incorporated. With the mixer on low speed, gradually add the flour. Stop the mixer, scrape down the sides of the bowl, and then beat on low speed just until well blended.

Spread the batter evenly in the prepared pan, smoothing the top. Bake the cake until golden brown, well risen, and beginning to pull away from the sides of the pan, about 1 hour and 10 minutes. A skewer inserted into the center should come out clean. Let cool in the pan on a rack for 5 minutes, then invert the pan onto the rack, lift off pan, turn the cake right side up, and let cool completely.

(continued next page)

To make the compote, put the sugar and water in a saucepan over medium heat and bring to a simmer, stirring to dissolve the sugar. Add the kumquats, cover, and adjust the heat to maintain a gentle simmer. Cook until the kumquats are tender, 15 to 20 minutes, uncovering occasionally to stir and to spoon out any seeds that have floated loose. (Ignore the tiniest seeds, which aren't bothersome.) When the fruit is soft, uncover and simmer until the compote is reduced to about 1 cup. Let cool until just warm. Pick out any more loose seeds, and stir in a few drops of brandy if desired.

Serve the pound cake in thin slices with a spoonful of the warm compote alongside. Pass the whipped cream separately.

SERVES 8

Note: To measure the flour properly, sift it first, then scoop it into a measuring cup, mounding it slightly. Level with a knife.

Vinegar by the Drop

I grew up in the Italian part of Switzerland, so even though my maiden name is Kellenberger, I have always felt at home among the Romans, the Tuscans, and the *marchigiani*. We Italians and quasi-Italians have many of our best times around the table. That's where new ideas surface and are considered and discussed. Certainly one of my crazier ideas—a costly one, as it happens—was hatched over dinner.

In the early 1990s, Bob and I often got together with friends who also had strong ties to Italy: Dante Bini, a famous architect, and his wife, Adria; Maria Manetti Farrow and her then-husband Stephen; and John Traina, a debonair socialite who collected Fabergé cigarette cases and was married to Danielle Steel. Good friends, good wine, a simple dinner in the kitchen: the best prosciutto to start, then pasta, *involtini, formaggi e frutta*. In those days, a bottle of *aceto balsamico tradizionale* was often on the table, and it was fabulous with whatever you put it on, from soup to strawberries.

Stephen and I were the interlopers, the only non-Italians. When Maria, a Florentine, met Stephen, she was married to someone else. Stephen was a student at UC Berkeley, a great-looking blond fellow studying abroad, and he came to her house in Florence looking for work. She hired him to do some gardening, but then she looked him over and they fell in love. He was several years younger.

Maria didn't speak English well when she moved to San Francisco with Stephen, but she was gorgeous and had that charming Italian accent, so how could you resist? She got a job at Joseph Magnin, the department store, in the Gucci department, and the sales must have shot up because the Gucci family gave her the rights to distribute Gucci accessories in North America. She got a big settlement when the company let her go years later. Then she worked for Fendi and did well with its products. Maria is a businesswoman, and she loves numbers as much as fashion.

Dante grew up in Modena and knew a lot about balsamic vinegar, which his family had made for generations. He claimed to have a recipe written in 1720 on sheepskin, as closely guarded as the gold in Fort Knox. In the 1960s, Dante designed, among other things, a circular inflatable house called a Binishell. The construction is all automated, so the house can be built in less than a day—invaluable in disaster areas.

We were drinking a very good Robert Mondavi Cabernet Sauvignon that night. It was from 1977—a drought year, so the wine had a fully concentrated perfume and taste. I suppose we had a bit much of it and were ready for adventure. What about making our own *balsamico* here in Napa Valley? Dante was ready to share the family recipe. We would be four partners: Dante, Maria, John, and me.

Now balsamic vinegar is an opus, and we had to get all the necessary parts together. Maria offered her round barn in Oakville. We decided that each of the four partners would purchase a *batteria*, the collection of wooden barrels that you need for authentic *balsamico*. We ordered them from

Viva l'aceto Balsamico
di Napa!
Marzo 3- 1995
Wappo Hill

Mozarella affumicata
in foglie di radicchio

Spumante
della casa

finocchio e funghi su crostini

Risotto con pomodoro
e carciofi
con spruzzo di aceto Balsamico

Chardonnay
Riserva 1992

Anatra arrosto
carote asparagi patate
Salsa di aceto balsamico

Merlot 1992

sformata di formaggio

Cabernet Sauvignon
Riserva 1991

ACETO
BALSAMICO
DI
NAPA

Compote di rabarbaro
gelato di crème brulée

Sauvignon Blanc
Botrytis 1983

il cuoco
Michael Chipchase

Francesco Renzi, the best barrel maker in Modena, and months later they arrived: oak, chestnut, acacia, cherry, ash, and mulberry barrels, carefully calibrated from large to small.

In the meantime, we read whatever we could find about *balsamico* and also contacted the ultimate authority, Renato Bergonzini. Would the *professore* come to Napa Valley and help us get started? We financed his entire journey. Bob and I put him up in our guesthouse. We rented a car for him and showed him Napa Valley hospitality. We took him to every good restaurant, arranged tours of wineries, and visited San Francisco. Did he bring his wife or girlfriend? I don't remember, but I do believe Renato Bergonzini had a good time with us.

Now we had to find the right must—the freshly pressed grape juice with skins and seeds—to start our production. In Italy, producers use Trebbiano grapes, which we didn't have in Napa Valley, so we decided on Merlot. Balsamic vinegar is not made from an aerobic fermentation like other vinegars. It is more like a grape sauce that is aged in a series of different woods.

Robert Mondavi Winery provided the first 150 gallons or so of Merlot must. Now we had to reduce it to about 31° Brix (about 31 percent sugar by weight). We divided the must equally, and in our four kitchens, in our crab pots or whatever big pots we had, we put it on to simmer. It had to be stirred constantly, so we set alarm clocks and had night watches. Each person stirred for two hours, and then the next shift came. It was like having a baby. The whole process took forty-eight hours.

This reduced must went into ordinary oak barrels for two days. Then we had to strain it through cheesecloth and transfer it into the biggest barrel in each of the four batteries. We covered the open tops with cheesecloth to keep the fruit flies away. It was as *garagiste* as you can imagine.

Then this fabulous salsa began to age. Like sherry in a *solera*, it had to be transferred from one barrel to another every year. With the quantity reduced from evaporation, it went into ever-smaller barrels each time. Dante was in charge, with Maria as the bookkeeper. She knew exactly how much was in every barrel.

The annual transfers at Christmastime were wonderful occasions. The four of us, with Bob as observer, would gather early in the morning in Maria's round barn and do the transfer with hand pumps, which took hours. Adria would be at home cooking, so by one o'clock, we could all go to the Bini house by the Napa River and celebrate. We would sit down to *una polentata*—polenta poured onto a big board—with two sauces, one with sausage, the other with *involtini*. Bob and I brought wine and the discussions began: What should we name the finished *balsamico*? How should we bottle it? What kind of bottle? We would have to design a label.

But in the meantime, trouble was brewing. We could not keep the fruit flies from the barrels. So a call was placed to *il professore*: What do we do now?

We had to filter the whole mess, he pronounced. Maria's barn was too open. Birds did their thing all over. So we would have to relocate the four batteries—twenty-four barrels in all.

Bob and I had a garden room under our house on Wappo Hill, and we all decided it would do. But once the barrels were installed, we realized the room was too damp. So Bob, in his magnanimous way, bought fans and dehumidifiers to try to take out the moisture. We really were stuck now, so we called Bergonzini again and invited him for another consultation.

He came and announced that the first filtering had not left the must clean enough. So we filtered again, added fresh must, and prayed a lot. Christmas came around again. Time for the transfer. And the *polentata*.

Lo and behold, after six years, we decanted our first *balsamico* from the smallest barrel. We each harvested about one pint of the precious stuff, and delicious it was. We had tastings with balsamic vinegars that cost at least fifty dollars an ounce. Ours was as good or better. But in the meantime, we realized that my cellar was far from perfect.

Dante lives in a century-old three-story house in St. Helena. He offered us his attic, which, according to Modena tradition, is the right place for *balsamico* barrels. In Modena, the *acetaie* (*balsamico* aging rooms) are usually on stilts or on higher floors—open to breezes, hot in summer, cold in winter. So we transferred the barrels yet again, this time up two flights of steps to the attic.

About every ten years, the barrels have to be emptied and washed with high-pressure hoses to remove the sticky sediment. Dante's house is right by the river, so when the time came to scrub our barrels, we carried them all to the river and rinsed them by hand on the riverbanks.

Decades later, the whole operation is still in Dante's attic, and we still keep it going, although we have made some labor-saving modifications. We now purchase the must, already reduced, from a local winery every year. And we have battery-operated pumps to do the transfers. No more laborious hand pumping, and I must say that makes everybody happy. We all remember squeezing that pump for hours.

How do I use this potent elixir? Sparingly. I like to mix it with good wine vinegar for dressing a salad. I love a few drops in mayonnaise and hollandaise. It's wonderful on strawberries, raspberries, and vanilla ice cream. I like a drop on a fried egg; on a steak, two drops; and a little drizzle on saffron risotto.

I found some tiny bottles to put the vinegar in, and we fill them by hand with miniature funnels. We sell a little bit in the gift shop at the Robert Mondavi Winery for $150 a bottle, and believe me, that price is a bargain. Every year, I give a few special friends a precious package with a handmade label. Bob would watch me do this and say, "There goes another thousand dollars." At least. But it is all a hoot, and if you saw our attic enterprise, you would think it is a wizard's laboratory where alchemy takes place. We lost one of our partners along the way—John Traina passed away in 2011—and although the rest of us are totally exhausted, we are also a bit proud of hand producing *la vera salsa balsamica di Napa.*

La Polentata *Creamy Polenta with Tomato Sauce and Panfried Sausage*

Adria Bini's polentata is always a highlight of the winter workday with my balsamico partners, when we transfer the precious condiment from barrel to barrel. This is my recipe, not Adria's, but the outcome resembles hers. Open a Robert Mondavi Merlot.

Kosher or sea salt

2 cups polenta

1 can (28 ounces) whole plum tomatoes,
    preferably San Marzano variety

3 tablespoons extra virgin olive oil

½ large yellow onion, minced

½ small bulb fennel, minced

2 large cloves garlic, minced

2 tablespoons minced Italian parsley, plus more for garnish

2 tablespoons minced fresh basil

1 tablespoon minced fresh oregano

Pinch of baking soda (optional)

1½ pounds (6 links) Italian fennel sausage (hot or mild)

5 to 6 tablespoons unsalted butter

1 cup freshly grated Parmigiano-Reggiano cheese

Bring 2 quarts water to a boil in a large, heavy saucepan over high heat and salt lightly. Gradually add the polenta while whisking constantly. When the mixture gets too thick to whisk, reduce the heat to medium-low and switch to a wooden spoon. Cook, stirring frequently, until the polenta is thick and creamy, 45 minutes to 1 hour. Add a little boiling water if the polenta gets too stiff for your taste, and adjust the heat so the polenta just bubbles. Season to taste with salt.

While the polenta cooks, make the tomato sauce. Puree the tomatoes in a blender or food processor, or pass them through a food mill fitted with the medium disk. Set aside. Heat 2 tablespoons of the olive oil in a large skillet over medium-low heat. Add the onion, fennel, and garlic and sauté until the vegetables are soft and sweet, 10 to 15 minutes. Add the tomato puree, parsley, basil, and oregano, stir well, and bring to a simmer. Adjust the heat to maintain a gentle simmer and cook until the sauce is thick and tasty, 30 to 40 minutes. Season to taste with salt. If the sauce still seems acidic, add the baking soda and simmer for another moment or two. Keep warm.

Prick the sausages in several places with the tip of a knife to prevent bursting. Heat the remaining 1 tablespoon olive oil in a skillet over medium heat. Add the sausages and cook until browned all over and firm, about 10 minutes. Transfer the sausages to a cutting board and let them rest briefly while you finish the polenta.

Add the butter to the polenta and stir vigorously until it melts. Remove from the heat and stir in ½ cup of the cheese. Taste for salt.

Pour the polenta onto a large wooden board and spread it into a layer 1 inch thick with a rubber spatula. Spoon the tomato sauce on top. Cut the sausages into chunks and arrange them on the polenta. Scatter the remaining ½ cup cheese on top and garnish with parsley. Serve immediately.

Serves 6

Saffron Risotto with Aceto Balsamico

Whenever I use my aceto balsamico, *I'm glad that my partners and I persisted with this sometimes dubious adventure. I forget all the trouble and expense when I get to share our handmade* condimento. *A trickle works miracles on a simple risotto;* balsamico *loves all that butter. Serve with Robert Mondavi Pinot Noir or Chardonnay.*

5 cups chicken broth

¼ teaspoon saffron threads, or more to taste

Kosher or sea salt

4 tablespoons unsalted butter

1 small yellow onion, minced

1½ cups Arborio or Carnaroli rice

⅓ cup freshly grated Parmigiano-Reggiano cheese

About 2 teaspoons *aceto balsamico tradizionale di Modena* or

   Aceto Balsamico di Napa Valley (see Note)

Put the broth and saffron threads in a small saucepan and bring to a simmer; cover and set aside for 30 minutes to steep. Taste and add more saffron if the flavor is not strong enough for you. Season the broth with salt. Just before you begin to cook the risotto, return the saucepan to medium heat and bring the broth to a simmer, then adjust the heat to maintain a gentle simmer.

Melt 2 tablespoons of the butter in a saucepan over medium heat. Add the onion and sauté until soft, 5 to 10 minutes. Add the rice and stir with a wooden spoon until hot throughout, about 2 minutes. Begin adding the hot broth ½ cup at a time, stirring often and adding more broth only when the previous addition has been absorbed. Continue until the rice is just al dente and you have used all or most of the broth, 18 to 20 minutes. The risotto should be moist and flowing, neither soupy nor stiff. If you need additional liquid, use boiling water.

Cover the pan, remove from the heat, and let stand for 3 minutes to allow the rice to finish cooking. Uncover and stir in the remaining 2 tablespoons butter and the cheese. Season to taste with salt.

Divide the risotto among warmed bowls. Top each portion with *aceto balsamico*, using about ½ teaspoon per serving. Serve immediately.

Serves 4

Note: You can purchase Aceto Balsamico di Napa Valley in the tasting room at the Robert Mondavi Winery.

Positively Paris

Bob and I made many trips to Europe on behalf of the winery, to host wine tastings or attend media events, especially after the debut of Opus One, our partnership with Château Mouton Rothschild. No matter where we went on the continent, we usually planned a few days in Paris at the end. That city is just too much of a temptation.

I was always flying about like a bird in Paris. The minute we landed, I would race to see where the exhibitions were, what was showing at Le Petit Palais and the Musée de l'Orangerie and the then-new Picasso museum. And, of course, I was not against a good walk up the rue du Faubourg Saint-Honoré to look at clothes. Bob, because he was fourteen years older, needed more rest. Within ten minutes of checking into our hotel, he would find a masseuse. I didn't mind at all because then I felt guilt-free about going shopping. And I am not 100 percent sure that he enjoyed the museums.

We stayed in many nice hotels, but Le Bristol, in the heart of the city, was a favorite. In the morning, I would sometimes just take off and walk to Place de la Concorde. I loved having my croissant and coffee in a bar, standing up.

I clearly remember one springtime visit when the chestnut trees were in bloom, and the weather was lovely, and it seemed as if every Parisian was in a good mood. Near the hotel was a vendor selling bags of fresh cherries, the enormous Griotte variety that specialty shops carry, preserved in brandy. The price was extravagant, but I had to have some. I gave the man the equivalent of twenty dollars, and I think I got only about ten cherries.

That same morning, Bob and I went to a little bistro on the Champs-Élysées run by the nephew of Gaston Lenôtre, the famous pastry chef. I don't recall whether we were having just coffee or a little lunch, but we heard English being spoken at the next table. A nod, a pleasantry, and soon there was recognition. We were talking with Frank Prial, the eminent wine columnist for the *New York Times*.

Frank had a residence in Paris and many of his *Times* stories were filed from there. We chatted and laughed and, on parting, Frank said, "Why don't you come to my place this evening for drinks and then we'll go out to dinner somewhere?"

Frank's apartment was on the Left Bank, and he was sure that we would never find it. So he gave us an address for the taxi driver and instructions to wait at the taxi kiosk. He would come fetch us between seven thirty and eight o'clock, and we would walk together to his place. The taxi deposited us at the designated spot, and after Frank appeared, we starting climbing the steep, narrow street to his flat.

About halfway up, Bob started to fidget. He was patting his pants pockets and frantically probing his jacket. This frantic little dance might have been funny if I had not known what was coming.

"I left my billfold in the taxi," he announced. Money, traveler's checks, credit cards, passport—all gone.

Believe me, this was not the first time. Bob had left billfolds behind in St. Petersburg, in Ho Chi Minh City, in London. He even dropped his wallet

in Calistoga once; it fell out of his pocket, but somebody found and returned it.

By now I knew the ropes. We would be spending the next morning at the American embassy, filling out paperwork to get Bob a new passport.

We retraced our steps to the taxi kiosk to see if the wallet had possibly fallen on the ground. Bonne chance. Our little dinner group began climbing the hill again, but Bob would not leave the kiosk.

"I'm waiting here," he announced. "The taxi driver is going to come back and bring me my billfold."

Everybody laughed. "Bob, this is Paris," someone said. "Do you really still believe in fairy tales?"

So we all trudged up the hill and left Bob down there, waiting. Frank had a lovely flat, and he opened some Champagne. But I wasn't at all comfortable, thinking of Bob standing alone at the kiosk, looking up and down the street. So I took my little handbag and announced, "I'm going down to keep Bob company."

Robert Mondavi did not have a negative bone in his body. He always saw the positive side. And because he was so honest himself, he trusted everyone. Many of his most important contracts in life were sealed with a handshake. He wasn't naive; he just expected that others would be as much of a straight dealer as he was. Not surprisingly, he was sometimes disappointed, but his outlook didn't change. If I ever spoke ill of someone, Bob would look at me crossly. He never doubted that people were fundamentally good.

As I approached the kiosk, I saw my husband waving his arms at me, so I began to run toward him. And when I reached him, there was Bob, jumping up and down and yodeling, "Look! He came back and brought me my billfold untouched, just as I told you he would." I could hardly believe it. The only person more astonished was the attendant at the kiosk. But that's the way it always was around Robert Mondavi. He believed … and it happened.

❧

ACKNOWLEDGMENTS

Margrit gratefully acknowledges the advice and encouragement of her painting teacher, Gail Chase-Bien.

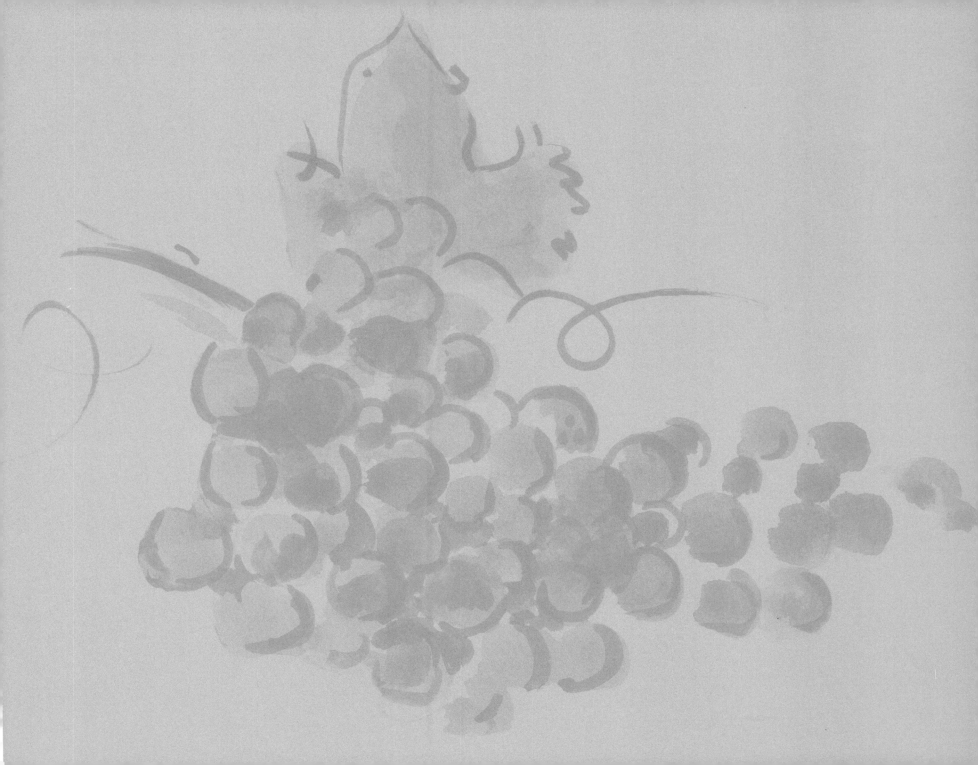